$4.00

THE GOOD SHEPHERD ALMANAC

SOW THE WORD...
HARVEST CHARACTER

*A year of devotions for the
growing Christian*

D0173849

KENTON K. SMITH

STANDARD
PUBLISHING

Cincinnati, Ohio

© 1998 by Kenton K. Smith
All rights reserved.
Printed in the United States of America.

Edited by Jim Eichenberger
Cover design by Barry Ridge Graphic Design
Interior design by Robert E. Korth

Published by The Standard Publishing Company, Cincinnati, Ohio
A division of Standex International Corporation

05 04 03 02 01 00 99 98   5 4 3 2 1

ISBN 0-7847-0766-9

Preface

Among the bright moments our family has enjoyed in the midst of Indiana's harsh winters are those that were spent thumbing through seed catalogs. The colorful illustrations of vegetables, flowers, and shrubs provided a welcome contrast to the bleak landscape outside our window. The promises of abundant yields made us eager to sink our fingers into spring's soil.

Part of the enjoyment resulted from our plans to grow something different each season. Once we grew three colors of string beans (and were later amazed when they all turned the same color in the cooking pot). On another occasion we planted chicory, just to see how it developed. Then there was the time we tried raising peanuts. Only one peanut reached maturity. Needless to say, we did not bother roasting it.

One aspect of gardening never came to mind when we browsed delightedly through those catalogs. We did not think about the hard work, the sweat, the blisters, the aching body, and the other negative features of the project. But when spring arrived, we were quite willing to endure these in order to grow the vegetables we dreamed of harvesting.

Farming and gardening require hard work. This is a fact we accept. But what about spiritual farming and gardening? Are we prepared to undertake the hard work necessary to be successful in this kind of enterprise?

When I speak of spiritual farming and gardening, I am, of course, referring to the many passages of Scripture that compare spiritual life and labor to agricultural activities. Jesus' parable of the sower, recorded in three of the Gospels (Matthew 13, Mark 4, Luke 8), is one of the more familiar of these. Paul's listing of "the fruit of the Spirit" in Galatians 5:22, 23 may come to mind. In Galatians 6:7-9 we find the familiar counsel about sowing "to please the Spirit" and the assurance that "we will reap a harvest if we do not give up."

In the following pages, I will discuss these and other similar Scriptures. For the time being, however, let us look at a statement Paul made to the Thessalonians that does not have such an obvious agricultural connection. In 1 Thessalonians 2:13, Paul spoke of "the word of God, which is at work in you who believe." Notice what Paul says: The Word of God *works*.

Now think for a moment of simple garden seed. It also works. Once it is planted in the soil, it germinates, sends shoots upward and roots downward, forms a plant, and ultimately bears fruit.

But we human beings work with that seed. We till the ground and break up the clods before we plant. After we plant, we cultivate, water, and fight off the insects and other pests. Then, at last, we harvest.

We must be willing to work with the Word. In this book we will examine some spiritual counterparts to the various steps in the agricultural process: spiritual plowing, sowing, cultivating, and watering.

The Word of God is a working word. Are you ready to prepare for the harvest?

Ken Smith, 1998

Some Pointers on

PLOWING

In his parable of the sower, Jesus described four types of soil, which represent four types of hearers of the Word.

To some extent, we are all hardened path soil (Matthew 13:3, 4, 19). Even when we are open to God's Word in most matters, we probably still have areas of hardness in our hearts. For example, we may enthusiastically seek to grow in faith, love, peace, and similar spiritual graces but balk when challenged to give ourselves to Christian service. Or we may be quite willing to develop our ability to evangelize within our own community but resist involvement in the missionary enterprise. Hardened soil must be plowed before we plant.

What is our "unplowed ground"? Let us look briefly at three kinds of hardened soil that exist in the hearts of most people.

Plowing up pride—First, we must work at plowing up pride. Even the best Christians still have some pretensions and some areas of inner resistance to God that require a rigorous breaking up.

Fortunately, the Word of God can serve as a plow by challenging our pride and calling us to humility. We must obliterate any traces of humanistic pride that will hinder the growth of God's Word in us.

Plowing up doubt—Once we have plowed up our pride, we need to work at plowing up doubt. God's Word commands, "But when he [the one praying] asks, he must believe and not doubt, because he who doubts is like a wave of the sea, blown and tossed by the wind. That man should not think he will receive anything from the Lord" (James 1:6, 7).

When we approach God's Word, we must make it our aim to break up doubt and to shatter it into insignificant pieces. That is what the plow does to the earth's crust, and that is what we must do to the unplowed ground of our hearts and minds.

Plowing up stubbornness and impenitence—Finally, we must plow up stubbornness and impenitence. Paul told his readers in Romans 2:5, "But because of your stubbornness and your unrepentant heart, you are storing up wrath against yourself for the day of God's wrath, when his righteous judgment will be revealed."

Are you covering up a sin? Are you refusing to repent? Are you clinging to a habit, a relationship, an attitude, or a set of values that you know is displeasing to God? Then you have some serious plowing to do before God's Word can take root within you and bring growth and blessing.

Have these discussions of common unplowed ground given you an insight into areas of hardness and resistance within your own heart? If so, we will soon give you opportunity for extensive plowing.

Some Suggestions on

SOWING

He answered, 'The one who sowed the good seed is the Son of Man'" (Matthew 13:37).

Jesus was the sower of the Word during his earthly ministry. In a sense, Jesus is still the sower of the Word, because it is he who has given us the valuable seed we find in the pages of our Bible.

After his ascension, Jesus left the actual responsibility of sowing the word to apostles, prophets, preachers, and teachers. We could refer to these people as "undersowers." They serve under the Master Sower himself, implanting the seed of his Word into human hearts.

Consequently, it is our responsibility to be present in congregations and classrooms where these undersowers can plant the seed into our hearts. We also need to "humbly accept the word planted in [us], which can save [us]" (James 1:21).

But we must not leave the responsibility of sowing God's Word in our hearts entirely to others. Hosea 10:12 says, "Sow *for yourselves* righteousness." Likewise, Galatians 6:8 indicates that we have a personal responsibility to be "one who sows to please the Spirit." In other words, although we will always need the help of undersowers who can plant the word into our hearts and minds in a powerful and pointed way, we must never neglect our personal responsibility to sow the seed of God's Word in our own lives.

Finally, when we read and study the Bible for ourselves, we need to keep our goal clearly in mind. If we do such reading only as a kind of religious exercise or merely to "score some points" with our creator, the seed will not do us any good. But it will produce a hundred, sixty, or thirty times what was sown if we approach our time with the Word as careful, diligent sowers, implanting it with the conscious aim of producing a harvest for God's glory.

Some Cues on

CULTIVATING

In the parable of the sower, Jesus refers to the seed sown among thorns. The people represented by this soil "hear the word; but the worries of this life, the deceitfulness of wealth and the desires for other things come in and choke the word, making it unfruitful" (Mark 4:18, 19).

Like any good farmer, we must watch out for weeds and root them out when they appear. Only then can the Word of God grow an abundant harvest in our lives.

Watching out for weeds—Worries and anxieties are two types of weeds. Perhaps we tend to be preoccupied with our health, our jobs, our property, our families, or our friendships. Such preoccupation leaves little room for the Word of God to grow and bear fruit us. That is why Peter urged his readers, "Cast all your anxiety on [God] because he cares for you" (1 Peter 5:7).

Our dreams of and desires for wealth are weeds. If we focus our thoughts on money and what it can purchase for us, it will be impossible for us to center our minds on God and his Word. Jesus emphasized this tension when he stated, "You cannot serve both God and Money" (Matthew 6:24).

What, then, are "the desires for other things" to which Jesus referred in Mark 4:19? Could he have been referring to those legitimate aspects of life that we often develop into obsessions? Sex, for example, is a wholesome part of the marriage relationship. But for many in our society, sex, separated from the wise restrictions God placed on it, has become a virtual focus of worship.

Similarly, some people seem to think and talk about sports constantly, while others are equally engrossed in cars or clothes or music or television or other amusements. These may be harmless in themselves, but they become gods in the way they demand a major sacrifice of people's time and attention.

Do we see any of the weeds described above springing up in our spiritual garden? What can we do about them?

Rooting out the weeds—Weed removal is a concern of every gardener. One may use the old-fashioned method of getting down on his knees and yanking the weeds up by their roots. Another gardener may be deft in handling a hoe, while still another prefers the option of utilizing a herbicide. Whatever the method, the gardener's motto is, "Death to weeds!"

In Colossians 3:5, Paul gives us some counsel that fits in well here: "Put to death, therefore, whatever belongs to your earthly nature: sexual immorality, impurity, lust, evil desires and greed, which is idolatry." If we are commanded to put such weeds to death, then surely God has provided a kind of "heavenly herbicide" to do it.

He has. The Bible is filled with warnings against various kinds of impure, unspiritual attitudes and habits. When we read, meditate upon, pray over, and put these warnings into practice, they act as a heavenly herbicide. If, for example, sexual lust is a weed hindering our spiritual growth, we can give Scriptures such as Exodus 20:17; Matthew 5:28-30, and Romans 13:14 our careful attention.

Combating weeds can be laborious and time-consuming. But the abundance of the harvest depends on it.

Some Words on

WATERING

As the rain and the snow come down from heaven, and do not return to it without watering the earth and making it bud and flourish, so that it yields seed for the sower and bread for the eater, so is my word that goes out from my mouth: It will not return to me empty, but will accomplish what I desire and achieve the purpose for which I sent it" (Isaiah 55:10, 11).

In this famous passage, God compares his own Word to rain. Therefore, if we give conscientious attention to the Word, it will not only serve as seed capable of growing spiritual graces within us—it will also function as the water that helps the seed to grow.

In addition to watering the seed in our own lives, God's Word will also spill over into the lives of others. Isaiah also writes:

"If you spend yourselves in behalf of the hungry and satisfy the needs of the oppressed, then your light will rise in the darkness, and your night will become like the noonday. The LORD will guide you always; he will satisfy your needs in a sun-scorched land and will strengthen your frame. You will be like a well-watered garden, like a spring whose waters never fail" (Isaiah 58:10, 11).

These verses are part of a magnificent chapter that describes the blessedness of those who minister to the needs of those around them. Our spiritual garden will be well-watered when we give priority to ministering to others. They may be politically or spiritually oppressed; they may suffer hunger of the body or of the soul. Either way, we are obligated to help them.

The best kind of watering for a cultivated field or garden is the intermittent rainfall that provides adequate moisture without washing away the soil. We need to water our spiritual garden this way. Memorizing brief passages of Scripture and recalling them often is an effective means of nourishing the crops we plant.

Our spiritual garden need never suffer the ravages of drought. We have the means of obtaining the rainfall that will keep it healthy and fruitful.

The Good Shepherd

Almanac

A DAILY GARDENING PLAN

The actual almanac for which this book is named follows. I have listed in it seed for fifty-two spiritual crops. These crops represent a variety of Christian aims, attitudes, habits, and practices. They do not constitute an exhaustive list of all that it means to be a Christian, but they do provide a good, basic starting point for spiritual growth.

Growing crops takes time and concentrated effort, in both the natural and spiritual realms. That is why this almanac is designed for you to devote an entire week to each crop. I would suggest the following schedule for this process.

Sunday—Each chapter begins with a brief introduction, describing the need for the character trait or practice of the coming week. Read this introduction to familiarize yourself with the crop you will be planting in the days to come. Spend time in prayer, asking God to bless your gardening efforts.

Monday—Before we sow, we must plow. When you read the plowing Scripture, picture your mind and heart as a vast field in which there is always more unplowed ground to break up and cultivate. Concentrate upon making your life more receptive to adding an additional godly attitude or habit.

Tuesday—I have carefully selected the fifty-two sowing passages. They seemed to me to be the most appropriate for describing the spiritual attitude or habit that the reader needs to develop. Study the sowing passage for each week thoroughly on Tuesday.

Wednesday—Study the first of the two cultivating passages. Although we have planted our crop for the week, our job is not over.

Thursday—Study the second of the two cultivating passages. Notice how some cultivating passages deal with specific "weeds," negative attributes we must eliminate in order to grow the positive trait.

Friday—The watering references are all very brief, easily memorizable segments of Scripture. This fits well with the concept of watering. After reading this section of the chapter, jot down this memory verse on a small card or on the "Notes" page for the week. Refer to it throughout the day.

Saturday—Continue to water by memorizing the Scripture you wrote down yesterday. Pause a few times during the day to test your retention. Then, like recurrent showers, these words will refresh and contribute to growth.

I sincerely hope that you will praise and pray your way through each week during this study. Plow, sow, cultivate, and water the seed of God's Word in your heart, mind, and life each week of this year.

K. S.

Week 1

Growing the crop of

A BIBLICAL VIEW OF HUMANITY

Glory to man in the highest, for man is the measure of things." So goes the humanistic view of humanity. If we can be properly educated, put in a position of economic advantage, purified of the pernicious influences of religion and superstition, then we will supposedly be capable of establishing an ideal society on earth. Such a viewpoint has no basis in reality. Evil exists among the educated and the uneducated alike. Economic prosperity often leads to greed for greater prosperity. Freedom from religion often means a liberation from any objective moral system, contributing to the breakdown of civilization. How desperately we need an emphasis on the biblical view of humanity and the sense of dependence on God that such a view promotes!

Plowing
Read Jonah 2:7-9.

This was part of the prayer Jonah offered while inside the great fish. Judging from Jonah's behavior after he was rescued from the great fish, this prayer must have been uttered in penitence. In the next chapter we see Jonah ready to complete the mission to Nineveh that God had earlier assigned him. The Lord went to extreme measures to bring Jonah to the point of submission to his will. Is he dealing in a similar way with us? Let us thank God for the sometimes tough means he uses to bend us to his will. Let us pray that we will allow those tough measures to soften us rather than to harden us.

Sowing
Read Psalm 8:1-9.

We are small, and we should not "get too big for our britches," because God is infinitely greater and wiser than we are. The psalmist was able to keep his smallness in mind by contemplating the heavens, and we may profit by doing the same. Such a practice will generate within us an appropriate humility and an amazement that God has such a high regard for us. Let us thank God for the "visual aids" he has provided in the heavens to help us keep ourselves in proper perspective.

Let us pray that we will remember to acknowledge the majesty and excellency of God in the midst of our human accomplishments.

Cultivating
Read Genesis 1:26-31; 2:7.

Neither a soulless machine nor a mere animal nor an insignificant speck of life in a vast universe—each of us is rather the unique creation of God, made in his own image. We were made to be masters over our environment, not in the humanistic, self-sufficient sense, but as stewards responsible to our creator. Let us thank God for this biblical emphasis on our uniqueness and specialness as human beings. Let us pray that we will exercise in a responsible way our rule over the earth and its other creatures and that we will keep in mind our role as stewards of God's creation.

Cultivating
Read Ecclesiastes 12:1-7.

We are more than deteriorating physical bodies. Solomon, in highly figurative fashion, depicts the ravages of age upon the body, then reminds us that this body is destined to return to the dust. But there is a light at the end of this gloomy summary: "the spirit returns to God who gave it." Let us thank God for the knowledge that our sometimes pain-racked, weak, aging bodies are only vessels for an eternal soul. Let us pray that we may treat our God-given bodies with respect and regard our God-given souls with even greater care.

Watering
Read John 3:16, 17.

The word "whoever" in this passage reminds us that God does not play favorites. His love is not limited to the favored few, nor are his promises reserved for some special elite. He loves each and every one of us—we are all favored, and we are all special in his sight. The key is, will *we* choose to be part of that "whoever"—those who respond in faith to his love? Let us thank God for John 3:16, the Bible's "golden text," that points us to the undeniable fact of God's love for every one of us. Let us pray we may believe that God loves us in spite of all the reasons we can call up as to why he should not.

NOTES

Week 2

Growing the crop of

A SERVANT SPIRIT

It is early Sunday morning. As Joe and Jane Christian get themselves and their children ready for church, what are they thinking? "I hope people are friendly today—I've had a rough week, and I need a lift!" "I hope they sing some of my favorite hymns and the preacher preaches on one of my favorite Scriptures." Does the average believer attend church preoccupied with the idea of "What am *I* going to get out of it?"

From Jesus' standpoint, it should be the opposite. We should say, "What can I say or do to make it a better day for others? How can I serve my brothers and sisters in Christ?" By sowing the following Scriptures, we can reproduce such a servant spirit within us.

Plowing
Read 1 Chronicles 22:17-19.

I t is not uncommon to say, "I'm going to put *my heart and soul* into this project." But do we devote our hearts and souls to seeking and accomplishing the Lord's will? Or are we distracted by a variety of sinful desires and worldly hopes? The Israelite leaders were challenged to devote themselves to building the temple; let us devote ourselves to building God's spiritual kingdom. Let us thank God for the glorious challenge of building his kingdom. Let us pray that we will learn to concentrate our attention and energy into doing his will.

Sowing
Read Philippians 2:1-11.

W hat a magnificent passage! What a Savior we have, one who was willing to be a suffering servant! And "your attitude should be the same as that of Christ Jesus." Our attitude can become the same as Christ's if we will take the time to meditate on this passage and let Jesus' example inspire us. Then "selfish ambition" and "vain conceit" will fade away, and "in humility [we will] consider others better than [our]selves." Then we will "look not only to [our] own interests, but also to the interests of others." Let us thank God for Jesus' amazing example of servanthood. Let us pray that Jesus' humble, self-giving character may be reproduced in us.

Cultivating
Read Romans 12:3-16.

E ach of us has gifts, talents, and abilities that we should put to use in our service in the church. And as we use these gifts, we must not relish our authority or nourish our pride but minister to the specific needs of our brothers and sisters. Let us thank God that he has given us personal resources to use in ministering to others. Let us pray that we may recognize our resources and put them humbly and wisely to work for the glory of God and the benefit of our fellow believers.

 ## Cultivating
Read Mark 10:35-45.

The modern reader feels a measure of disgust over the disciples' constant scrambling for superiority over one another, but their behavior is often reproduced today. It is still a very human tendency to seek power and position, to desire a place in which we can feel superior to others. Jesus, however, emphasized the greatness of humble service and pointed to his own example of dedication to sacrificial ministry. Let us thank God that we do not have to imitate the world's anxious struggling for power. Let us pray that we will obtain a clearer understanding of the greatness of Christlike service and learn to devote ourselves to it.

 ## Watering
Read 1 John 3:16.

Can we sincerely say that we lay down our lives for our Christian brothers and sisters? Or do we help them only if it is convenient to do so? Do we serve one another only when it does not cost us anything? The kind of service John is describing here seems to be rare, but it should not be. Jesus Christ's willingness to lay down his life for us should inspire us to similar sacrifice. Let us thank God for the beauty of this verse and the challenge it lays before us. Let us pray for an understanding of what it means to lay down our lives for our brothers and sisters and for the courage to follow through.

NOTES

Week 3

Growing the crop of

ANTICIPATION FOR CHRIST'S RETURN

An old gospel song begins, "Jesus may come today! Glad day! Glad day!" Do we believe that, and if so, do we feel such a sense of joyful expectancy? Or must we answer such questions in the negative?

So many years have passed since Jesus left this earth; so much wickedness has flourished, seemingly unnoticed and certainly not halted by the Almighty; so few of our fellow believers exhibit any keen awareness of the possibility of Jesus' returning today— how can *we* generate such an anticipation?

Only God's Word can keep us alert to the promised coming again of our Savior and living Lord. Let us grow this crop of anticipation this week.

Plowing
Read 1 Chronicles 28:9.

What does the Lord find when he searches our hearts? Is he pleased with every motive behind our thoughts? Would we dare join the psalmist in praying, "Search me, O God, and know my heart" (Psalm 139:23)? God knows us thoroughly, so it is wise for us to be open to him and to repent of all our hidden sins. Let us thank God for the fact that, although he knows our every thought and motive, he still loves us. Let us pray that we will learn to welcome his gaze into our innermost being.

Sowing
Read Acts 1:1-11.

Jesus will "come back in the same way" that he departed this earth. That means visibly and spectacularly. For the apostles, the angels' words of assurance must have been very welcome. Without doubt they cherished the promise of Jesus' return during the days following his ascension and during the trials that came afterward. That promise also fortifies us against the temptations and pressures we must face. Let us thank God that we serve not only a crucified and risen Savior but a coming Lord. Let us pray that we may, like the apostles, be about the Lord's business as we await his return.

Cultivating
Read Matthew 24:36-51.

Nothing is inherently wrong with "eating and drinking, marrying and giving in marriage." But this must have described the total preoccupation of nearly all human beings in Noah's time. Today, a great many people are completely caught up in earthly affairs, unaware that Jesus Christ is coming again. We Christians also may be tempted to relax our watch, to become careless and spiritually idle. Jesus put a good deal of emphasis on our need to watch and to be ready for his return. Let us fix his admonitions in our minds and hearts. Let us thank God for the various biblical warnings to prepare ourselves for Christ's return. Let us pray that we may avoid being lulled into forgetfulness and idleness by the flow of daily routine.

Cultivating
Read 1 Thessalonians 5:1-11.

Under cover of darkness, the thief breaks into your house. But even more than the darkness, it is the unexpectedness of this break-in that makes it work. Someday a vastly more significant unexpected event will occur: the return of Jesus Christ. We Christians should not be caught unexpectant and unprepared. We should not be spiritually asleep. Let us thank God for the challenge of being "alert and self-controlled." Let us pray that we may keep a keen sense of expectation for Christ's return.

Watering
Read Revelation 22:20.

A gospel song pleads, "Wait a little longer, please, Jesus" and seeks for "a few more days to get our loved ones in." This raises the question of whether or not we should echo John's prayer for Jesus' soon return. After all, we undoubtedly know many people whose eternal fate would be sealed if Jesus were to return today. We should pray for those people and labor to persuade them to turn to Christ, but we should also pray for Jesus Christ's triumphant return. Let us thank God for the dramatic way the Bible closes with this prayer. Let us pray that we may share John's sense of anticipation for the Lord's return.

NOTES

Week 4

Growing the crop of

APPRECIATION FOR JESUS' PASSION

The term "passion" is frequently used in reference with Jesus' sufferings and death. Here, however, we employ it to refer to the passionate, wholehearted dedication Jesus demonstrated in fulfilling his mission. Although he knew the same temptations and needs that we know, Jesus passionately refused to let his desires distract him. He was undeterred by hunger, a quest for acceptance, or a fear of suffering.

If we are to be his genuine followers, we must possess the same kind of passion for the mission to which he assigns us. Let us sow into our hearts and minds a thorough acquaintance with the following passages that describe Jesus' passion. Then let us look for the growth in us of that spirit of our Lord and Leader.

Plowing
Read Psalm 95:6-11.

This passage points back to Exodus 17. The Israelites had seen God's works in Egypt, when the ten plagues forced Pharaoh to release them from slavery. They experienced an amazing deliverance from Pharaoh's chariots at the Red Sea, where they crossed on dry ground between walls of water. They received a miraculous supply of quail for food, and the manna began to appear on an almost-daily basis. And yet, when their need for water grew desperate, they did not trust God to supply it. Instead, they complained and tested the Lord's patience. Moses called the site of this crisis "Massah" (testing) and "Meribah" (quarreling). Are we also guilty of forgetting God's past supply of our needs and falling into a spirit of complaint? Let us thank God for abundant blessings in times past. Let us pray that we may put away the tendency to doubt and complain when we must wait on him to supply our needs.

Sowing
Read Luke 22:39-46.

What happened in the garden? Was Jesus tempted to flee and avoid the sufferings he knew lay ahead? Did he hope that through prayer he might find some other way than the cross to fulfill his mission? One thing is certain: Jesus endured a tremendous amount of emotional stress where "his sweat was like drops of blood falling to the ground." We know that Jesus triumphed over whatever struggles he faced there, for he remained in the garden until the betrayer and the arresting party arrived. Let us thank God that Jesus withstood the pressures he encountered in the garden. Let us pray that we may likewise withstand any pressures that would divert us from our God-given missions.

Cultivating
Read John 6:60-71.

With a human nature like ours, Jesus must have appreciated popularity. In spite of this, Jesus was not willing to allow the desire for popularity to keep him from speaking the truth people needed to hear. His discourse on the bread of life, recorded earlier in this chapter, was such a truth. We see that truth cost him in terms of popularity. Let us thank God that Jesus chose faithfulness to his mission over the lure of popularity. Let us pray that we may have the courage to make a similar decision.

Cultivating
Read John 2:13-17.

We often affirm that Jesus was a man of peace, but in this passage we see him involved in what could accurately be called violence. Of course, we are not told that Jesus used the whip on human beings. It was not the kind of violence that people inflict on one another with guns or knives. But in spite of his generally peaceful character, Jesus could not overlook an irreverent use of the temple. Let us thank God for Jesus' demonstration that peace does not mean ignoring evil. Let us pray for the wisdom to know when to make peace and when to wage war against evil.

Watering
Read John 4:34.

We could reverently point out that Jesus never needed to go on a diet. Treating his taste-buds and stuffing his stomach was not a matter of priority to him. Accomplishing his Father's work was. Of course, Jesus certainly recognized that a properly nourished body was advantageous in serving God. But how we need to catch some of Jesus' passion, so that eating, sleeping, recreation, and every other activity become secondary to accomplishing God's work! Let us pray that we may establish such a priority in our own lives.

NOTES

Week 5

Growing the crop of

APPRECIATION FOR JESUS' PERSON

It is distressing to see how Jesus is portrayed today. He is the focus of irreverent humor, the victim of distorted theology, and the subject of perverted works of "art." His name is callously thrown about as a favorite term for idle cursing.

We may be perplexed by the world's attacks against someone we hold so dear, but we should not be shocked. Jesus was subjected to ridicule and blind opposition in his days on earth, and he prophesied that many in the world would continue to hate him. We must keep alive in our hearts and on our lips the real Jesus, the One whose divine character transcends every human distortion. The Scriptures for this week will lead us to appreciate Jesus for who he was, is, and ever will be.

Plowing
Read Luke 18:9-14.

Where are we in this parable of Jesus? Is the Pharisee's tendency to compare himself favorably to others familiar? Are we inclined to pray, "God, I thank you that I am not like others—homosexuals, abortionists, pornography addicts, thieves, and murderers"? Each of us must rather demonstrate the attitude of the tax collector: "God, have mercy on me, a sinner." Praise God that we can speak of ourselves as sinners saved by grace, but we must nevertheless recognize that we are sinners. Let us pray that we may eliminate any trace of Pharisee-like hypocrisy and that we may develop more fully the humble attitude of the tax collector.

Sowing
Read Matthew 16:13-20.

Who do you say that Jesus is? Have you, like Peter, been so impressed by his personality, his teachings, and his mighty works that you would be quick to exclaim, "The Christ, the Son of the living God!"? How wonderful it is that we can, in a sense, look over the shoulders of the disciples and witness the unmistakably divine character of Jesus' personality! Let us thank God for Peter, often impetuous but on this occasion remarkably perceptive. Let us pray that the good confession—that Jesus is the Christ, the Son of the living God—may be a dynamic reality in our lives.

Cultivating
Read John 7:45-52.

The temple guards were given a simple assignment: to arrest Jesus. (See John 7:32.) When they returned empty-handed, they did not excuse themselves by admitting to fear of the crowds around Jesus. They simply said, "No one ever spoke the way this man does." It requires no reading between the lines to detect their sense of wonder at this remarkable Galilean. If only the chief priests and Pharisees had opened their minds and hearts, they too could have felt the same wonder. Let us thank God for this brief account and the way it demonstrates the power of Jesus' personality. Let us pray that our sense of wonder may continuously grow as we ponder the magnificence of our Lord and Savior.

Cultivating

Read Luke 7:36-50.

Jesus was ever and always approachable, as this story wonderfully illustrates. The woman sensed that, although the Pharisee would reject her for her sinful life, Jesus would not. So she approached Jesus in a humble, loving, and obviously

penitent manner. Jesus accepted her attention and extended forgiveness to her. And at the same time, in a remarkably gentle way, Jesus reproved the Pharisee for his lack of graciousness. Let us thank God for Jesus' love for sinners of all kinds. Let us pray that we may be so deeply impressed with his merciful love toward us, and that we may view the sinners around us in the way he did.

Watering

Read Matthew 11:28-30.

What an invitation! Jesus is addressing us, for we are all weary and burdened and longing for rest. How can anyone read or hear these words and not want to fall down in adoration before him? How can anyone refrain from following a Lord who so gently and lovingly calls to discipleship? Let us thank God for the universal appeal of these words. Let us pray that we, along with other human beings, may learn to bear his easy yoke and light burden.

NOTES

Week 6

Growing the crop of

APPRECIATION FOR JESUS' POWER

All hail the pow'r of Jesus' name!" So we sing in the words of one of our more stirring hymns. "Power" is a word that fits Jesus better than any other person who has lived on earth.

Think of the military heroes—Alexander the Great, Julius Caesar, Genghis Khan, Napoleon—they are all puny beside Jesus. Think of the intellectual giants—Plato, Aristotle, Marcus Aurelius, Galileo. Consider the giants of industry, the power brokers of today and days gone by, the movers and shakers, the high rollers, the empire builders, and tycoons of every sort. All pale in comparison to Jesus. Let us sow an appreciation for him as the most powerful person in all history.

Plowing
Read Luke 15:11-24.

This is a lengthier passage than we have generally been considering, but it is difficult to shorten. We can focus, however, on the son's words to his father when he returned: "Father, I have sinned against heaven and against you. I am no longer worthy to be called your son." Can we sincerely say to God that we are not worthy? Are we not rather inclined to feel that we deserve God's favor because we are such good persons, conscientious workers, and sacrificing parents? Let us thank God for the lost son's father, who illustrates the willingness of our heavenly Father to forgive his unworthy children. Then let us pray for an eye-opening experience that will strip us of any pretense that we are worthy of God's favor.

Sowing
Read Matthew 9:1-8.

We marvel at the brevity, simplicity, and beauty of this account. In four short sentences, Jesus met the challenge of his critics. In effect, Jesus said, "Let me show you the power and authority I possess. Then you decide who I am." Only the most hardhearted and stubborn critics could fail to be convinced by such a display. Let us thank God for Jesus' acts of healing and the divine power they demonstrated. Let us pray that we may be filled with awe and stirred to ever-greater praise by the power of our Savior and Lord.

Cultivating
Read Matthew 12:22-29.

What a contrast we see here! The people were astonished by Jesus' miracle and ready to acclaim him as Messiah. But the Pharisees were obviously angered by the miracle and quick to attribute it to the devil. It is still true today that some readers of the Bible are awed by Jesus' displays of miraculous power, while others are interested only in explaining them away. Let us thank God for the reality of Jesus' miracles. Let us pray that we may be made more deeply aware that Jesus has power greater than that of the devil.

Cultivating
Read Luke 8:22-25.

Reading the Bible in the security of our living rooms or bedrooms, it is difficult to envision the terror the disciples felt as they were engulfed in the storm. We try to imagine the fishing boat tossed about like a toy on the waves. We struggle to picture the crashing waters filling up the boat, threatening to swallow up the vessel and its passengers. And we strain to capture a mental image of the Master at the moment he reined in the storm with a brief command. All this mental exercise is worth it, if we can feel a bit of the amazement the disciples

felt. Let us thank God for the power Jesus demonstrated over nature. Let us pray for the strengthening of our faith through pondering such accounts as this one.

Watering
Read Acts 10:38.

This is what power is for: "doing good." Jesus' mighty works were never mere spectacles, intended only to move people to amazement. They were directed toward healing, assuring, blessing, and strengthening human beings. Whatever power we possess—the power of our personality, the gift of persuasive speech, our financial assets, and our position—should be directed toward the same ends. Let us thank God for the beauty of Jesus' deeds of kindness and power done to humble human beings. Let us pray that we may likewise invest our resources into ministering and doing good to those around us.

NOTES

Week 7

Growing the crop of

APPRECIATION FOR JESUS' PRESENCE

Jesus Christ's earthly life concluded almost two thousand years ago, but he is still present with us. We are not able to see him, hear him, or touch him as his contemporaries did, but we are still privileged to know him and experience his nearness.

How are we going to respond to that privilege? In what ways should we be honoring the presence of the living God in our lives?

We should respond with humility, excitement, gratitude, commitment, and love. By giving prayerful attention to the passages for this week we can increase our awareness of his presence with us and thus intensify our appreciation for that privilege.

Plowing
Read Proverbs 28:13, 14.

Human beings are very skilled in the art of concealing sins. We may pretend that they do not exist or call them "errors in judgment," or "products of our childhood environment," or "acts justified by our living in an oppressive society." We may take the viewpoint that, since no harm was done, there is nothing to worry about. But Solomon tells us that concealed sins will find some way of breaking out with painful results. Let us thank God that he is compassionate and forgiving and that we have, therefore, no reason to hide our sins. Let us pray that we will develop the habit of confessing and renouncing every sin.

Sowing
Read Luke 19:1-10.

We may consider the story of Zacchaeus, the "wee little man," as suitable mainly for children. But this delightful account should touch us all. See how Jesus' presence in the home of Zacchaeus changed the man! A tax collector, a traitor to his people, possibly a cheater and oppressor— Zacchaeus became a man dedicated to honesty and generosity. Do we qualify as a Zacchaeus, or do we know someone else who does? The presence of Jesus can transform any Zacchaeus. Let us thank God for Jesus' willingness to associate with those who were unpopular. Let us pray that Jesus' presence in our lives will make us open to any "Zacchaeus" we encounter.

Cultivating
Read John 12:1-8.

Although Judas Iscariot was in the company of Jesus, he was preoccupied with his greed. It is one of the facets of the personality of Judas that puzzles us. He spent perhaps three years in close fellowship with Jesus, but somehow he failed to recognize that he was with the

Son of God. His doubtful discipleship stands in stark contrast with the devotion of Mary. Let us thank God that, although Jesus is not here in the flesh today, we are able to enjoy his presence. Let us pray that we may not be preoccupied with things, as Judas was, and thereby fail to appreciate our Master's presence.

Cultivating
Read Luke 10:38-42.

Distracted Martha and devoted Mary we may call them. Like Martha, many modern-day followers of Jesus are so busy doing things *for* him that they are distracted from enjoying fellowship *with* him. Jesus' refusal to reprove Mary indicates that Mary had found the right balance between serving Jesus and stopping to enjoy his presence. Let us thank God for the privilege of serving Jesus, working in the church and doing good deeds in his name. Let us pray that we will be careful, like Mary, to save time for Jesus to teach us and strengthen us through his abiding presence.

Watering
Read Matthew 18:20.

It is not necessary to have two or three thousand, or even two or three hundred, or even two or three dozen. Just two or three people meeting in Jesus' name are assured of his special presence. This promise covers a family gathering for devotions, a small group of friends getting together for Bible study and prayer, and the tiniest congregation of Sunday worshipers. Let us thank God that we do not need great numbers or an elaborate setting to have Jesus within the circle of our fellowship. Let us pray that we will be ever conscious of his presence in these gatherings.

NOTES

Week 8

Growing the crop of

AWARENESS OF GOD'S GOODNESS

The bombing of a federal building in Oklahoma City . . . mass graves discovered in Bosnia . . . a powerful earthquake in Kobe, Japan . . . deadly plane crashes and automobile accidents . . . the daily litany on the news of murders and suicides—how, some ask, can God be good and allow such tragedies to occur?

While this is an extremely difficult question to handle, it is clear that we must place our faith in the goodness of God. The alternative—to regard the Almighty as cruel, capricious, or unable to control the twists and turns of fate is unthinkable. The Bible provides us with some solid help in recognizing the underlying goodness of our creator.

Plowing
Read Obadiah 1-4.

The pride of the Edomites had deceived them. They were sure that their natural fortifications "in the clefts of the rocks" would keep them safe from any enemy, but the Lord would soon cause them to be brought down. Pride still deceives nations and individuals. If we live in the dream world of our own self-sufficiency, we must awaken. Let us thank God for giving us constant reminders of the perils of godless pride. Let us pray that we may profit from the examples of the Edomites and other proud people in the Bible whom God brought down.

Sowing
Read Psalm 34:8-14.

Taste and see that the Lord is good." Give God a chance and learn just how good he is. Many people never give God a chance to demonstrate his goodness. They look at the trials and disasters the human race encounters and carelessly conclude that no good God would allow such circumstances to exist. If we will taste, we will learn that, in spite of the existence of enormous evil, God *is* good. Let us thank God for the invitation to experience his goodness. Let us also pray that we will perceive the divine goodness lying beneath even the most terrible tragedies.

Cultivating
Read Psalm 25:4-15.

This is one of the most beautiful of the psalms in its spirit of confidence in God's goodness. Another prominent element in this psalm, is God's activity as teacher and instructor of human beings. We could put these two emphases together and look for God to teach us his goodness. With our tendency to be negative about God when we experience hard times and disappointments that would be an appropriate quest. Let us thank God for showing us his ways, guiding us, teaching us, and forgiving us. Let us pray that we may become more teachable and receptive regarding the fact of his eternal goodness.

Cultivating
Read Mark 10:17-22.

Isn't Jesus good? Of course he is, even if he seems to imply here that he is not. God is good, and Jesus is the Son of God. Elsewhere (John 10:11) Jesus acknowledges that he is the good shepherd. But the point to be noted in Jesus' exchange with the rich young man is that no mere human being is good. The young man was not good, in spite of his adherence to the law. No person that we think of as being exceptionally good deserves that description. "No one is good except God alone." We must lay

aside all human examples and standards when we try to contemplate God's goodness. Let us thank God for his goodness and for the goodness of Jesus Christ, which set the true standard of goodness. Let us pray that we may better realize the limitations of human goodness and the unlimited splendor of God's goodness.

Watering
Read Psalm 119:68.

We saw it earlier, and here it is in briefer form: acknowledging God's goodness is a key to teachableness. The psalmist's confession is a valuable addition to our mental arsenal against doubt and despair. If we memorize and frequently recall this verse, we will be able to affirm with the poet Whittier: "To one fixed trust my spirit clings, I know that God is good." Let us thank God for the psalmist's brief but powerful prayer. Let us pray that we may vanquish any doubts regarding the goodness of God.

NOTES

Week *9*

Growing the crop of

AWE AT GOD'S MAJESTY AND GLORY

When comedian George Burns died at age one hundred, someone sent him a posthumous tribute addressed to "the only God I'll ever know." That was in reference to Burns's portrayal of God in the *Oh, God!* movies.

Those movies were an example of the continual human tendency to remake God in our own image. Instead of looking at God to understand ourselves, we look inward, trying to understand God. We must avoid this tendency and appreciate God for who he is: the majestic and glorious creator and sustainer of the universe. Implanting the Word, with its revelation of such an awesome God, is essential. May this awe grow from the seeds we plant this week.

Plowing
Read Psalm 63:1.

Are we in earnest about our quest for God? Or is religion merely a matter of convenience and curiosity for us? There was no question about the earnestness of David, the psalmist. If we must admit we have only been dabbling in religion, toying with faith, playing games with God, now is the time to repent and become an earnest seeker. Let us thank God for the fact that David, though greatly flawed, gave us a vivid example of earnestness toward God. Let us pray for guidance in making an honest appraisal of our spiritual commitment and in changing whatever is lacking.

Sowing
Read Psalm 19:1-6.

Do you want to behold the glory of God? Then look up! God's glory and majesty are displayed in the vastness and the splendor of the heavens. In a great hymn based on this psalm, Joseph Addison said of the heavenly bodies: "In reason's ear they all rejoice,/ and utter forth a glorious voice,/ forever singing as they shine,/ 'The hand that made us is divine.'" Let us thank God for the visual aids he has placed in the heavens to demonstrate his glory. Then let us prayerfully aim to become godly stargazers, looking up from the trials of this earth to the celestial reminders of God's ultimate rule.

Cultivating
Read 1 Chronicles 29:10-13.

What a paean of praise to our majestic and glorious God! We would do well to incorporate David's words frequently in our public and private worship. No more wonderful theme could occupy our tongues and our minds. Contemplation of God's majesty and glory lifts us high above the occasional monotony, pain, and frustration of earthly existence. Let us thank God for the remarkable revelation he gave to his servant David. Let us pray that these words may lift us heavenward when earthly burdens drag us down.

Cultivating
Read Psalm 96:1-13.

Nearly three thousand years later, we still need this reminder: "For all the gods of the nations are idols, but the LORD made the heavens." It is fashionable today to regard all religions as being of equal value. But it is an affront to our majestic and glorious God to put him on the same level as Allah of the Islamic faith or the deities of Hinduism. He alone is God! He alone is Creator! He alone is worthy of our praise! Let us thank God for the insistence of his Word that he alone is God. Let us pray that we will have the courage to speak out for this truth in an age of religious compromise and confusion.

Watering
Read Revelation 4:11.

Think of it—God created all things! He designed the solar system and earth's ecosystem. He gave the sun and stars their light and tiny firefly its light. He made the moon to circle the earth and electric current to move in its circuits. He has sent the fleecy clouds on their journey across the skies and the woolly sheep to graze in meadows. How greatly is God's glory exhibited in his creation! Let us thank God for the manifestation of his glory in all creation. Let us pray that we may become godly observers of nature, marveling at God's power and wisdom in all he has created.

NOTES

Week 10

Growing the crop of

BOLDNESS AND COURAGE

The Christian leaders who have exerted the greatest influence on the world in modern history were people of boldness and courage. Think of Martin Luther, John Knox, John Wesley, Fanny Crosby, Alexander Campbell, Dwight L. Moody, Mother Theresa, and Billy Graham. They trusted in the God of all power to embolden them and to calm their fears. What a great legacy!

If we are to make the kind of impact we need to make on the present generation, it will take more men and women of exceptional boldness and courage. And it will take biblical truth planted within human hearts to produce a harvest of such women and men. Let us start this week.

Plowing
Read Amos 7:7-9.

The Israelites did not measure up to what God expected of them. How do we measure up? Would the Lord's plumb line show us "true to plumb"? We need regular reminders that it is not our standards of measurement that count, but the Lord's. If we have worked out our own personal moral code, our behavior may consistently conform to that. But it is essential to check ourselves out against the only complete and perfect standard—the Word of God. Let us thank God for showing us clearly in the Bible what he expects of us. Let us also pray that we may never be deluded into thinking that any standard of behavior can substitute for the biblical standard.

Sowing
Read Acts 4:5-20.

"Unschooled, ordinary men" can speak with an unconquerable boldness if they have God's Spirit dwelling in them. Peter was not only an unschooled, ordinary man—he was also the one who had denied Jesus three times after his arrest. What a difference the Holy Spirit made in him! Let us thank God that, whatever our level of education or intellect, we can still take a bold and courageous stand for Jesus Christ. Let us offer a prayer of surrender so that the indwelling Holy Spirit can reproduce such a boldness in us.

Cultivating
Read Psalm 27:1-3.

David is saying, "Bring on any conceivable calamity. I can face it, for I have courage through God my helper." The man who had stood up to Goliath in battle could make such a claim, for he had experienced divine aid in a time of tremendous challenge. How can we acquire such a spirit of boldness and courage? Surely one way is to internalize this powerful passage. We need to memorize it, meditate upon it, and make it a fixture in our minds. Let us thank God for the courage he gave David and for the realization that he can do the same for us. Let us pray that David's God-given attitude be ours as well.

But let us also pray for a clearer perception of how all effective leadership and all genuine encouragement comes from God.

Cultivating
Read Deuteronomy 31:1-8.

The loss of a leader can lessen people's courage. Moses was about to lay down the burden of leadership he had carried for a long time. Here we see him unselfishly endeavoring to bolster the courage of the Israelites in general and of Joshua, his successor, in particular. His message was, "Human leaders will come and go, but the Lord remains with you. His leadership never fails." Since we lose human leaders occasionally today, we need that message as much as the Israelites did. Let us thank God for Christian leaders and the encouragement they give us.

Watering
Read Proverbs 28:1.

What does it mean to be "as bold as a lion"? Since a lion fears no other beast, it must mean that we will fear no one but God. It means we will stand our ground in spite of the threats of the ungodly. It means we will sound forth the truth like the fearless roaring of a lion. What amazing things could we accomplish for God with that kind of boldness? Let us thank God for this vivid illustration of the boldness we should have. Let us pray that we may replace fearfulness, timidity, and hesitancy with this impressive boldness.

NOTES

Week 11

Growing the crop of
BROTHERLY LOVE

What would happen if we were to ask a number of passersby on a busy city street for their one-sentence definition of love? Many would describe it as a wonderful emotion; some would depict it in terms of sacrifice; probably only a few would acknowledge it as a gift from God.

It is clear from the biblical viewpoint that love is not a natural human response. It may be natural for us to cherish and protect the people close to us. It may be a part of our human nature to form a romantic attachment with a person of the opposite sex. But the unselfish, outreaching, all-encompassing kind of love to which the Bible calls us is a precious gift vouchsafed to us by God's Spirit.

Plowing
Read Joel 2:12, 13.

The Jews had a custom of expressing penitence or horror over sin by tearing their clothing. While clothing was more precious then than now, it was nevertheless a comparatively easy way of demonstrating sorrow for sin. So the Lord said through Joel, "Rend your heart and not your garments." This is a vivid way of describing the painful process of sorrowing over our ungodly attitudes and habits and then laboring to remove them. Let us thank God that the pain of penitence gives way to the comfort of cleansing. Let us pray for the courage to face and endure whatever suffering is necessary in order to free ourselves from besetting sin.

Sowing
Read 1 John 4:7-16.

Dear friends, since God so loved us, we also ought to love one another." John writes so simply but so beautifully of God's love and our love. We could try, in our own strength, to imitate God's love. We could expend time, money, and effort in sacrificial labors for our fellow human beings. But unless it is truly God's love that shines through us, these labors will accomplish little. Let us utilize this passage to sow the authentic love of God into our hearts. Let us thank God for demonstrating vividly through Jesus Christ his love for us. Let us pray that our feeble, self-serving attempts at love may be swallowed up in the abundance of his own love abiding in us.

Cultivating
Read Luke 10:25-37.

The priest and the Levite in this famous parable have plenty of modern-day counterparts. People do not want to be bothered with their neighbor's needs; they do not wish to get involved with their neighbor's problems. But the Samaritan received Jesus' commendation because he demonstrated the kind of love God's ancient command calls on all of us to demonstrate. Let us thank God for this Samaritan and his inspiring acts of neighborliness. Let us pray that God will never let us be content with an "I-don't-want-to-get-involved" attitude.

Cultivating

Read 1 Corinthians 13:1-13.

We could call verses 4-7 "the positives and negatives of love." Notice how many times the words "not" and "no" appear. We are shown what love does *not* do as well as what it does. These verses provide us with a kind of checklist by which we can test the genuineness of our love.

How do we measure up to the positives and negatives with our love in our families, in our churches, and in the world at large? Let us thank God for providing us this divine checklist. Let us pray that his Spirit will transform our sometimes selfish love into the tremendous godly love described here.

Watering

Read John 13:34, 35.

Where is this unique brotherly love that identifies us as Jesus' disciples? Our devotion to one another in the church should far surpass what people can find in a social club, a circle of fellow employees, or an informal gathering of cronies in a tavern. What makes that love so unique, that devotion so special, is its imitation of Jesus' love for us. Let us thank God for this challenging command Jesus has given us. Let us pray that his own love will thrill us, inspire us, and fill us so that we may respond with a brotherly love that will impress all who witness it.

NOTES

Week 12

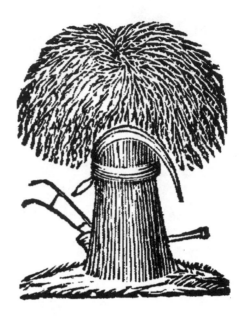

Growing the crop of
CHEERFULNESS

T he song leader says, "Let's see some smiles out there!" The congregation responds by affixing happy expressions on their faces. Some sourpusses, however, deepen their frowns, as if to register their resentment at being prodded into a false cheerfulness.

This raises some questions: "Should a Christian wear a continual smile? Should a Christian be able to generate a sincere smile on command? Is a frowning Christian a poor witness for Jesus Christ?" However we answer these questions, it is clear that Christians have cause for cheerfulness in spite of their circumstances. It is also clear that we can sow and cultivate a godly cheerfulness.

Plowing
Read Isaiah 30:15-18.

How foolishly we resist God's invitation to turn from sin and to trust in him! The Israelites resisted, looking for safety in swift horses. We seek our security in money, education, political influence, and weapons. But it is futile to rely on anything or anyone other than our sovereign Lord. Notice how he longs to be gracious unto us and compassionate toward us. Why should we resist such a God? Let us thank God for offering us the one dependable means of safety—resting in him. Let us pray that we will perceive the ultimate inadequacy of every earthly form of security and that we will learn how to wait for God.

Sowing
Read Proverbs 12:25; 15:13, 15, 30; 17:22.

Cheerfulness does us good, and it also ministers to others. There is nothing wrong with doing good to ourselves. Cultivating cheerfulness is a way of developing a healthy mind and body for the Lord to use. Radiating good cheer can benefit others by reminding them of Browning's observation that "God's in his heaven—all's right with the world!" Let us thank God for all the healthy benefits a cheerful spirit can produce. Let us pray that we may learn to resist the "gloomies" and to insist on the "cheerios" instead.

Cultivating
Read 2 Corinthians 9:6-11.

What a goal—to be "a cheerful giver." And Paul lists some excellent reasons in this passage for cheerfulness in giving. We will "reap generously," "abound in every good work," and "be made rich in every way." All of this is in contrast to our tendency to think of giving as painful or bothersome. Let us thank

God for the good he accomplishes through the generous giving of his people. Let us pray for a vision of what our giving can accomplish, and let us pray that we may thereby discover real cheer in it.

Cultivating

Read Acts 27:13-26.

It is difficult to imagine the despair that must have gripped the passengers aboard Paul's ship. Caught in the jaws of a monster storm, unable to see the sun and stars by which to navigate, resigned to ultimate destruction—that was their situation. *The King James Version* has Paul exhorting them to "be of

good cheer." At first his counsel must have seemed like the ravings of a fool. But the time came when Paul's shipmates responded positively to his cheerfulness (see verses 33-36). Like Paul, we should aim to be bearers of cheer in the darkest, most hopeless occasions. Let us thank God that an angel of the God we serve is ever standing beside us. Let us pray that we may develop an unquenchable cheerfulness as a witness to those around us.

Watering

Read John 16:33.

Here is another place where the *King James Version* has "be of good cheer"—this time instead of "take heart." Either way, Jesus speaks of an attitude that refuses to allow tribulation or trouble to defeat us. We could speak of this verse as a call to "positive thinking," but it is positive thinking grounded in the reality of who Jesus is. Let us thank God that Jesus gives us abundant cause for cheerfulness. Let us pray that we will lay hold of that cheer that overcomes every trial.

NOTES

Week 13

Growing the crop of

CHRISTIAN CITIZENSHIP

It is true that "our citizenship is in heaven" (Philippians 3:20), but for a time it is also in a nation here on earth. Our earthly citizenship should consistently reflect our higher citizenship. If human laws come into clear conflict with God's, then "we must obey God rather than men" (Acts 5:29). But when people rule in harmony with God's authority, we must obey them. Besides keeping the law, we must always work to bring the values of our higher kingdom into our present world—the values of love, mercy, truth, righteousness, and justice.

God's Word can change entire civilizations. This week, let us plant seeds of Scripture that will yield a harvest of better citizenship and, ultimately perhaps, a more righteous nation.

Plowing
Read Matthew 5:3.

We do not have to be poor in order to be poor in spirit. Perhaps it is sometimes easier for people who experience material poverty to humble themselves before God, but that is certainly not always the case. Whatever our economic level, we must understand that we come before God as weak, foolish sinners, utterly dependent on his grace. Let us thank God for the material wealth we enjoy as well as for our education and our physical skills. Then let us pray that in spite of our level of wealth and success we will see ourselves as weak and foolish in God's sight.

Sowing
Read Romans 13:1-7.

The government is not our enemy, nor are its agents our foes. We may be disappointed and even disgusted with certain governmental leaders and their policies, but they are still God's servants. Certainly we must object whenever government makes laws that conflict with God's will. But we must remain submissive to just laws and respectful of the governing authorities. Let us thank God for showing us that his authority underlies all human government. Let us pray for guidance in influencing our government and our society to adhere to the will of God.

Cultivating
Read Matthew 22:15-22.

Jesus did not endorse any taxpayer's revolt. Of course, he surely disapproved of many of the uses to which the Romans put tax money. The taxes helped pay for the Roman army's oppressive reign over many peoples. Some of the revenue went into financing state-supported pagan worship. Perhaps some of it was channeled into

underwriting the mainte-
nance of public brothels. Jesus
was aware of the abuses of
the rulers of his day, but he
could not focus on these now.
He gave first priority to
building a better kingdom—
God's eternal kingdom. Let us
thank God that we can be
glad for the results of much of
the tax money we pay: public
schools, road construction
and maintenance, public
parks and recreational areas,
law enforcement and the
court system. Let us pray that
we may be responsible
Christian taxpayers who do
not lose sight of our alle-
giance to a higher kingdom.

Cultivating
Read 1 Peter 2:13-17.

Many of our fellow citi-
zens are blind to the
blessings of liberty
and the obligations of freedom. We Christians are
warned not to "use [our] freedom as a cover-up for evil."
But others exploit freedom
and resent government inter-
ference with their various
"rights." Our government is

far from perfect, but it is far
better than what Peter experienced. We should show other
citizens the kind of freedom
united with responsibility to
which Peter referred. Let us
thank God for his call to a
responsible, respectful citizenship within human society.
Let us pray that we may so
conduct ourselves today as to
"silence the ignorant talk of
foolish men."

Watering
Read Proverbs 14:34.

Today's political catch-
words are "freedom,"
"unity," "power,"
"progress," and "choice."
Imagine a candidate for office
running on a platform of
"righteousness." That seems a
strange suggestion, yet it is
undeniably true that freedom,
unity, power, and progress are
dependent on righteousness.
We can make our nation
stronger and more prosperous
by praying for and calling for
righteousness. Let us pray
that we may be able to con-
vince our fellow citizens of the
excellency of righteousness
and the disgracefulness of sin.

NOTES

Week 14

Growing the crop of

CHRISTIAN STEWARDSHIP

People frequently ask, "Do you own your home?" Even if your name is on the deed to the house you live in, the answer is actually no. God owns your home and the furniture in it. He owns your car, your clothing, your food supply, and everything else. In addition, God is the owner of all your talents, skills, and abilities. We are merely the stewards or caretakers of a few of his possessions. Surrendering ownership of material goods to God is especially difficult in our materialistic culture. When we fully accept that the value of our lives has no relationship to our inventory of "toys," however, we save ourselves a lot of confusion and turmoil. Let us sow this principle into our hearts and minds as we study the Scripture this week.

Plowing
Read Psalm 42:1, 2.

Have you ever been really thirsty? Was there a time when your craving for water was so urgent that it dominated your thoughts? Would you ever have gladly traded valued possessions for a glass of water? Surely this is the kind of thirst the psalmist had in mind when he spoke of thirsting for God. We need to give our souls what they are really thirsting for. Let us thank God for that soul thirst that only he can satisfy. Let us pray that we will be wise enough to avoid trying to satisfy that ultimate thirst with anything less than God.

Sowing
Read Matthew 25:14-30.

Where do we find ourselves in this parable? Are we like the five-talent man, using our abundant gifts in fruitful service? Are we like the moderately gifted two-talent man, making the most of our limited gifts? Or are we like the fearful, hesitant one-talent man, failing to invest our gifts, however large or small, in our Master's cause? Obviously, we must prayerfully avoid falling into this last category. Let us thank God for our gifts for service, whether they be many or few.

Let us prayerfully aim to be "good and faithful" servants, utilizing every gift to its utmost effectiveness.

Cultivating
Read 1 Corinthians 4:1-7.

What do you have that you did not receive?" We may say that we have worked our fingers to the bone and scrimped and saved in order to have what we have. But it is the Lord who gives jobs, the health and strength to work at them, and the wisdom to use well the wages we are paid. Therefore, we have good reason to see ourselves as his stewards. It is our privilege to be entrusted by him with both material and spiritual treasures. We must prove faithful to him. Let us thank God for the realization that everything we possess has been received from him. Let us pray for a firmer grasp of that realization.

 ## Cultivating
Read 2 Timothy 1:8-14.

God has made a priceless deposit to our account—the gospel. And we must be, like Timothy, good stewards of it. That involves guarding it from the temptations that would deplete our spiritual account and protecting it from the forces that seek to destroy it altogether. But it also involves testifying about it. Paul urged Timothy to join him in suffering for that testimony. He surely invites us as well to expose ourselves to possible sufferings as we speak out for Jesus Christ. Let us thank God for his entrusting to us the sacred treasure of the gospel. Let us pray for the Holy Spirit's help in guarding it and testifying about it.

 ## Watering
Read Exodus 20:17.

The grass is always greener on the other side of the fence. What belongs to our neighbor may look good to us, but it is foolish to covet any of it. God has given bountifully to us. We should cultivate a contentment with what we have and ponder how we may best use it for God's glory. Let us thank God for his goodness and wisdom in supplying our needs. Let us pray that we may eliminate the wasteful and dangerous distraction of yearning after what other people possess and that we may focus on using for God's glory what we already possess.

NOTES

Week 15

Growing the crop of

COMFORT

We will focus here on both the receiving and the giving of comfort. At certain times *we* need the comfort God and God's people offer. On other occasions we must commit ourselves to being God's messengers of comfort to suffering friends and acquaintances.

As we sow Scriptures that minister God's comfort in us and through us, it is well to ponder the meaning of the term. The Greek word translated "comfort" in several New Testament passages paints the picture of being called alongside of another person. Our English word conveys the idea of giving strength to someone else.

Let us aim to offer comfort like that.

Plowing
Read 2 Kings 22:18-20.

This was the prophetess Huldah's answer to an inquiry from King Josiah. Josiah had a responsive heart. How is your heart? Is it sluggish or distracted or pessimistic or rebellious? Can we make our hearts more responsive to God? Surely with the power of God's Word and the power of prayer, the answer is yes. Let us thank God for the example of Josiah, who, though ruling a proud and rebellious people, was nevertheless humble and responsive. Let us pray that Josiah's example will profoundly affect us and that his attitude of humble responsiveness will be reproduced in us.

Sowing
Read 2 Corinthians 1:3-7.

Why do you need comfort? Has someone dear to you died recently? Have you lost some precious items of personal property? Are you hurting over a failure in your job, your family life, or your work in the church? "The Father of compassion and the God of all comfort" can minister to whatever need you have. As Paul indicates in this passage, God often uses human beings to serve as his messengers and ministers of comfort. But we must be willing to let them serve us. Let us thank God that he offers a comfort to soothe the bitterest sorrow, to calm the most insistent questioning. Let us pray that we may accept the comforters God sends us and that we may also learn to be effective comforters.

Cultivating
Read Matthew 10:26-31.

A song made famous by Ethel Waters assures us that "His eye is on the sparrow, and I know he watches me." Sparrows and other birds do fall to the ground—we see them lying there on occasion. But it is nevertheless comforting to know that God is watching and providing for them and us. We need to be afraid of nothing other than our Father, and how can we be frightened of one who cares so much for us? Let us thank God for this reminder: every time we see a bird in flight or perched on a tree limb, it is a symbol of God's care for us. Let us pray that we may properly balance a fear of our Father with confidence in his comfort and care.

Cultivating

Read Revelation 21:1-5.

It is comforting to know that we shall soon be eternally comforted. When we suffer pain now, what a relief to know that pain will ultimately cease to exist! When we struggle now with grief and sorrow, what joy to realize that these things are soon to vanish! Let us keep our hope fixed on that great day when we shall see that "the

old order of things has passed away." That will help us through the present tough times. Let us thank God for the promise of heavenly, eternal comfort. Let us pray for a more consistent "heavenly-mindedness" in the face of our earthly trials.

Watering

Read Isaiah 66:13.

As a mother comforts her child"—what tender scenes do these words evoke! We think of the fretful infant finding comfort as well as nourishment at its mother's breast. We picture the toddler, hurt in a fall, but being soothed on his mother's knees. We envision the teenage girl, upset by a conflict at school, but calmed by her mother's embrace. God longs to comfort us like this, if we will just come to him. Let us thank God for the warm remembrance of a mother's comfort. Let us pray for an understanding of how the best features of parental love are magnified in God's caring love for us.

NOTES

Week 16

Growing the crop of
COMPASSION

People who are hurting may reject our pity but welcome our compassion. What is the difference? The person who pities stands on the outside looking in. The person who has compassion identifies with the sufferer's pain and deeply desires to alleviate it.

Perhaps this distinction is not really found in the meanings of the terms. However, it is certain that the way we have described compassion is an accurate depiction of our compassionate Christ. It is also the kind of compassion we must develop. Sensitive response to suffering was his way, and it must become ours.

The following passages will help us to reproduce Christlike, biblical compassion within us.

Plowing
Read Matthew 5:4.

The mourning Jesus spoke of here is obviously related to our sins and our sinfulness. It is possible to approach our sins by shrugging our shoulders and saying, "I'm only human. I make mistakes like everyone else." If we could see how much those sins grieve our heavenly Father, if we could perceive how much damage they do in terms of human suffering, then we would surely be moved to mourning. Let us thank God for demonstrating in Scripture the extreme seriousness of sin. Let us pray that our eyes may be opened to the ugly reality of sin as God sees it.

Sowing
Read Mark 1:40-45.

The leper mentioned in this passage is not described, but his appearance may well have been hideous. We know that leprosy is a disease that eats away at the body, resulting in the loss of fingers, toes, nose, ears, and other body parts. Today, other sicknesses often disfigure people. Their bodies may waste away; they become incontinent; they lose the ability to think clearly and express themselves rationally. Perhaps we are repulsed, but, like Jesus, we must have compassion. Let us thank God for Jesus' compassion toward the sick. Let us pray for the strength to move beyond our natural revulsion to the disfigurement of disease and respond with Christlike compassion toward the sick.

Cultivating
Read Mark 6:30-34.

This is how Jesus saw the throngs that surrounded him—"like sheep without a shepherd." That must be how he views today's mixed-up multitudes, and it is how we should view them. No wonder people cling desperately to their possessions and pleasures. They need a shepherd. Why do human beings immerse themselves in the misery of feuds, conflicts, and wars? They need a shepherd. What is the explanation for the unceasing appetite people have for alcohol, drugs, illicit sex, and occult religion? They need a shepherd. We should feel compassion for them and point them to the genuine Good Shepherd. Let us thank God that we have come to know him as a compassionate shepherd. Let us pray that we may replace any tendency to be harsh and judgmental with godly compassion.

Cultivating
Read Luke 7:11-17.

The scene that Jesus encountered at Nain was common then, and it continues to be all too common today. That day it was a mother mourning a dead son; at other times it has been children grieved over the death of a parent, a husband or wife desolate over the loss of a life partner, a group of people bereaved of a dear friend. We are surely not overstating the case when we say that Jesus'

heart goes out to these mourners as it did to the widow of Nain. And our hearts should respond in the same way. Let us thank God for the reality of his compassion when death takes away someone dear to us and let us pray that we may be vessels of God's compassion toward others who experience bereavement.

Watering
Read James 1:27.

The existence of nursing homes and children's homes in our time does not alter our obligation toward widows and orphans. No institution can ever provide all the care that a needy individual requires. We probably know of senior citizens or troubled young people who would be blessed by our personal ministry. So let us extend Christlike compassion toward them also. Let us thank God for his loving concern for the very old and the very young. Let us pray for an increasing awareness of the needs of the elderly and the young alike, and for the wisdom to minister effectively to those needs.

NOTES

Week 17

Growing the crop of

EFFECTIVE EVANGELISM

Let us sow Scripture so that we may become better sowers of Scripture. Evangelism involves friendliness, patience, boldness, and persistence, but it is first of all a matter of sowing the Word of God. What is our attitude toward the Scripture? Do we have a compassion for the lost? Do our lives reflect the power and righteousness of the God we proclaim? Are we prepared to speak to others about their deepest needs?

We can sow the characteristics of an effective evangelist by internalizing the passages listed for this week. And all our sowing of God's Word, in connection with all of the spiritual crops we endeavor to grow, will contribute to our effectiveness in harvesting precious souls for the glory of God.

Plowing
Read Jeremiah 3:11-13.

Have we been "faithless" as Israel was? Are we guilty of breaking faith with God by violating his commands and engaging in unholy deeds and thoughts? God may be frowning on us now but he wants to smile. If we will practice faithfulness and eliminate faithlessness, we can avoid that awful frown. Let us thank God for his call to faithfulness, righteousness, and holiness. Let us pray that we may develop a deep concern over God's frowning upon us and that we may learn to do what will gain his smile of approval.

Sowing
Read Colossians 4:2-6.

Eggs, popcorn, fresh vegetables—yes! But our *conversation* "seasoned with salt"? What does that mean? Some commentators suggest that it could refer to wit. That is an appealing thought. The use of tasteful humor can catch the attention of our hearers and make them more receptive to the serious truths we want to present. Let us thank God that because of Christ we have good reason to be cheerful, lighthearted, and witty. Let us pray for the wisdom to speak for Christ appropriately and appealingly to those who do not yet know him. Let us also pray that we may "know how to answer everyone" who questions us regarding our faith.

Cultivating
Read Acts 8:26-40.

The Ethiopian eunuch seems like the ideal candidate for salvation. He was a man concerned about religious matters and was open to further teaching of divine truth. He was willing to ask pertinent questions and listen to the answers. Finally, he was prompt to respond to the biblical call to obedience. Let us thank God that there are still "Ethiopian eunuchs" who hunger for spiritual truth and are willing to listen to biblical teaching. Let us pray that God will lead us to such persons and that we can tell them "the good news about Jesus."

Cultivating
Read John 4:1-26.

The Samaritan woman was so much like people we encounter today. There are individuals who love to "talk religion," and they are very opinionated about the subject. But if we can work past the outward veneer of religious palaver, we may find a person who is thirsting for the kind of spiritual realities only Christ can provide. Let us thank God that Jesus Christ gives the fully satisfying water of life. Let us pray that we will not only be able to discern the desperate thirst in the hearts of non-Christian friends and acquaintances but also be effective in leading them to the water of life.

Watering
Read 1 Corinthians 9:22.

Poet F.W.H. Myers has captured the evangelistic urgency Paul felt: "Then with a rush the intolerable craving shivers throughout me like a trumpet call/ 'O to save these! Perish for their saving! Die for their life! Be offered for them all!'" Paul's desire to bring others to salvation was so compelling that he was willing to "become all things to all men." Let us thank God for the sense of evangelistic urgency we already possess. Let us pray that it will grow like a trumpet call within us. Let us also pray for the insight to become all things to all people so that by all possible means we might save some.

NOTES

Week 18

Growing the crop of

EFFECTIVE RESISTANCE TO THE DEVIL

Forget the comic figure with the red suit, horns, and pitch-fork—the devil is real, and he is no laughing matter. Jesus took him seriously, and so must we.

Satan is not impressed with our intellect or education, our cleverness or eloquence, or our influence among our fellow human beings. Our best defense and offense against him lie in the Word of God.

Of course, the devil wants to snatch away the spiritual seed from our hearts (Matthew 13:19), and he is eager to sow his own variety of weeds (Matthew 13:25, 39). But we can begin with determination to sow and cultivate such scriptural truths as those listed for this week.

Plowing
Read Isaiah 8:19, 20.

Have you ever decided to seek guidance or help through astrology, spiritism, or some other form of the occult? It is a dangerous decision, since the Bible shows that the occult is part of the devil's realm. We should repent of such involvement in Satan's realm and make up our minds never to visit it again. We should also commit ourselves to inquire only of our God and of "the law and . . . the testimony." Let us thank God for his guidance and help, which make inquiry into the occult an unnecessary alternative. Let us pray that we may clear our lives of any contact with the occult.

Sowing
Read Matthew 4:1-11.

Surprisingly enough, Jesus wielded a sword! Of course, it was "the sword of the Spirit, which is the word of God." We will look at that description in our next Scripture. By his skillfully using of the Word of God to combat the devil's temptations, Jesus demonstrated the power the Word can give us in overcoming our own temptations. Obviously, we must learn the Word well, so that we will be "armed to the teeth" with it whenever Satan goes on the attack. Let us thank God for the devil-defeating power of his Word. Let us also pray that we may become expert "swordsmen" in wielding the Word as Jesus did.

Cultivating
Read Ephesians 6:10-20.

We are at war! The devil opposes a growing, spiritually prosperous church. He is throwing his full force against the church, determined to divide it and weaken it. He is waging war against individual Christians, seeking to destroy their discipleship and wipe out their witness. In this passage is the weaponry we must have in place to thwart the devil and his army. Let us thank God that he has not left us helpless before the hosts of wickedness but has provided an effective array of spiritual armor. Let us pray for each item enumerated that we may fit it securely in place and use it effectively against Satanic assaults.

Cultivating
Read 1 John 3:7-10.

The reason the Son of God appeared was to destroy the devil's work." We say, sometimes facetiously and sometimes at least semi-seriously, "The devil made me do it!" But with the powerful Son of God at work in our lives, the devil cannot *make* us do anything.

Jesus Christ can thwart every temptation, overcome every tactic, and repulse every attack of the devil, if only we will let him. Let us thank God for the crushing victory Jesus has already won over Satan. Let us pray that we may more fully realize how, with Jesus, we are ultimately on the winning side.

Watering
Read 1 Peter 5:8, 9.

The devil is no pussycat! He is a vicious, roaring lion, seeking to prey upon us. We must respect his power and beware of him. But in Jesus Christ we do have the power to resist him. Let us thank God that we are able to say no to Satan. Let us pray that we will be alert to discern when he is stalking us and prompt to use our power of resistance.

NOTES

Week 19

Growing the crop of

EFFECTIVE SERVICE

E ven people who exhibit skill and expertise in their chosen professions may regard themselves as "church klutzes." That is, they may stumble and falter and fumble when asked to serve as a leader, teach a class, help with visitation, or serve in some other way in the church. They approach their church-related duties with a measure of fear and trembling, and perhaps that is only proper. After all, the eternal destiny of the people we serve is at stake. On the other hand, if we serve with the power of the Holy Spirit and in harmony with biblical aims and attitudes, we should be able to surmount our stumbling tendencies. The following Scriptures will guide us into effective service.

Plowing
Read 2 Chronicles 30:6-9.

King Hezekiah sent this message throughout the land after the Assyrians had conquered the northern kingdom of Israel and sent most of its people into exile. The king made a remarkable promise: If the Israelites who remained in the land would return to the Lord, he (God) would enable their fellow Israelites in captivity to come back to their homeland. This would happen because "the LORD your God is gracious and compassionate." God also wants us to return to him, so that he may reverse some of the damage sin has done in our lives. Let us thank God for his graciousness and compassion. Let us pray for insight into ways in which we have drifted from the Lord and for guidance in making our return.

Sowing
Read 1 Peter 4:7-11.

Here is the purpose of Christian service: "that in all things God may be praised through Jesus Christ." Do we serve with the aim that God will receive all the glory? Because of our frail humanness, it is natural for us to hope for a measure of praise for ourselves, at least a small amount of personal glory. As we mature in Christ, one mark of that maturity will be service undertaken solely for God's glory. Let us thank God that we may bring him glory through our acts of service. Let us pray for that spiritual maturity that rises above self-seeking service.

Cultivating
Read John 13:1-17.

So, should we schedule a foot-washing service in our church? That would be missing the point of Jesus' teaching. Jesus was not commanding us to observe what would soon become an empty ritual. Instead, he wanted us to be alert for various ways in which we can render humble service to one another. Let us thank God for the way in which Jesus has provided us living examples of the kind of life we are meant to live. Let us pray for wisdom and guidance to find the modern-day parallels to foot-washing, the specific ways we can minister to one another's needs.

Cultivating
Read Galatians 6:1-10.

We are to be "do-gooders" in the best possible sense of that term. Without intruding into other people's business, we should do whatever good we can to neighbors, fellow workers, the needy, and everyone else. In addition, we are to do good especially to our fellow Christians, "those who belong to the family of believers." How can we restore those who have sinned? How can we carry other believers' burdens? How can we share good things with those who teach us? These are questions we must ask and answer. Let us thank God for opportunities to serve others, inside the church and outside of it. Let us pray that we may recognize the opportunities when they appear and act effectively upon them.

Watering
Read 2 Corinthians 4:5.

God's servants, Jesus' servants, servants of others for Jesus' sake— what a privilege to be such servants! It is vital that we fix this in our minds: "We are servants! I am a servant! I have been called to serve others in Jesus' name!" If we *see* ourselves as servants, it stands to reason that we will render more effective service. Let us thank God that we may call ourselves his servants. Let us pray that we may comprehend more fully what that means.

NOTES

Week 20

Growing the crop of

EFFECTIVE WORSHIP

B ible teachers and preachers occasionally point out that
"worship" is a shortened form of "worthship." In worship
we are to acknowledge God's worth or worthiness of our
praise and devotion. From the outset, then, worship should be
God-centered rather than worshiper-centered.

We tend to approach public worship on the basis of what's in
it for us. We think it should make us feel good, that we should
come away with a sense of being relieved, refreshed, and rejuve-
nated. That may well be a result of worship, but the primary purpose of worship is to offer our creator the adoration and exalta-
tion he deserves. Let us sow some Scriptures that will help us do
that.

Plowing
Read Lamentations 3:40-45.

This seems as much complaint as it is confession. In the same way, we probably mix complaint with confession from time to time. We may admit to sin but complain that the consequences of our sin are harder than they should be. Perhaps we tend to blame God for allowing us to be tempted in the first place. It is natural for us to complain, but we must beware of letting the complaint outweigh the confession. Let us thank God for his patience with our complaining. Let us pray for the assurance that God will forgive when we sincerely confess our sins.

Sowing
Read Psalm 99:1-9.

Exalt the Lord our God and worship." To exalt, according to the dictionary, is "to elevate by praise." How can we elevate God, who is the most high God? Perhaps the idea is that of lifting high his name, sending heavenward our praise to the God and Father of our Lord Jesus Christ. We must use our voices in worship, employing our lips and tongues to sound forth his praise. Let us thank God that we have voices we can use in worshiping and exalting him. Let us prayerfully devote our voices, lips, and tongues to such a purpose.

Cultivating
Read John 4:19-26.

How do we worship the Father "in spirit and in truth"? Jesus is clearly saying that worship is not confined to any one location. We can worship in the woods, on a lake, and atop a hill, but we should also worship in a church. True worship must come from our hearts, regardless of outward trappings. It must be humble, sincere, trusting, and obedient. Let us thank God that we may worship him at any time and in any place. Let us pray that we may more fully understand the implications of worshiping "in spirit and in truth" and worship accordingly.

Cultivating

Read Revelation 19:6-10.

Heavenly worship is "hallelujah" worship. That word, which is Hebrew for "Praise the Lord!", appears four times in Revelation 19. It demonstrates the excitement and enthusiasm of heavenly worship. And surely our earthly worship should be patterned after what is done in Heaven. In Revelation 19 we have multitudes and groups uniting in praise, and we can do the same with our hymn-singing. Many of our hymns cause us to say, "Hallelujah! Thine the glory," "Hallelujah, what a Savior!" and "Praise Him! Praise Him!" Let us thank God for the many examples of heavenly worship in Revelation. Let us pray that our church's worship may grow more similar to that heavenly worship.

Watering

Read Psalm 122:1.

The psalmist must not have been desperate to sleep in. He apparently had received no unexpected company. He did not have any television shows that kept him up late the night before. But even if such temptations had existed, they would have been unlikely to affect him. He was eager to go to the house of the Lord. We also should feel such eagerness to assemble together for worship. Let us thank God for the house of worship that we attend. Let us pray that we will find increasing delight in the worship opportunities it provides us.

NOTES

Week 21

Growing the crop of

GODLY FAMILY VALUES

The term "family values" has become a popular one in political debates and discussions. We have seen the entertainment industry make a fresh effort to provide movies and television shows that cater to the family.

But in all this recent focus on family values, one question remains unanswered: "Whose family values?" If we base such values on the teachings of popular psychology, on the agendas of politicians seeking re-election, or on moviemakers looking to increase profits, we will remain in confusion. The passages below will give us an excellent start on instilling God's family values— profoundly wise and eternally applicable principles for a successful home.

Plowing
Read Matthew 6:33.

We seek a wide variety of possessions, accomplishments, and experiences, but what do we seek *first*? It should be the kingdom of God and his righteousness. If any other seeking takes precedence over this, then we are engaged in a form of idolatry. We must say, "God first! Christ first! Faith first! Discipleship first!" Let us thank God for his call to put him first in our affections and our aims. Let us pray that we may become aware of anyone or anything that is becoming an idol to us and that we may move it to its proper place under God.

Sowing
Read Psalm 128:1-6.

Happy the home when God is there"—so begins one of our Christian hymns. And that statement is a summary of the sentiments found in this psalm. Among the blessings of the God-fearing home are a sense of purpose, the satisfaction of emotional needs, beauty and graciousness, growing children, and bright hope for the future. Let us thank God for his creation of the family and for his readiness to bless the godly family. Let us pray that we may contribute to the building of God-fearing, spiritually prosperous families.

Cultivating
Read Ephesians 6:1-4.

Some people look at this passage and pronounce it a hopeless ideal. They may lump it together with the family television shows of the fifties, such as *Leave It to Beaver* and *Ozzie and Harriet*. Obedient children, wise and patient parents—this just does not happen. But we answer, "Why not?" If we aim at family life "in the Lord" and "of the Lord" (note those extremely significant prepositional phrases), we can surely achieve strength and harmony in family life. Let us thank God for the biblical emphasis on godly family relationships. Let us pray that we may indeed center our family life "in the Lord."

Cultivating
Read Deuteronomy 6:1-9.

The Word of God was to be prominent in the Hebrew home. How can we make it prominent in ours? Posting Bible verses on walls, doors, mirrors, the refrigerator, and elsewhere may be helpful. This passage, however, pictures the home as a center for biblical teaching; instruction in the Word is to pervade all of family life. We need to have family devotions, not as a brief, periodic activity far-removed from other domestic affairs, but as timely and relevant instruction for life together. Let us thank God for the challenge of making the home a Bible school. Let us pray that we may learn to relate all family goals, plans, problems, and disagreements to the teaching of God's Word.

Watering
Read Proverbs 22:6.

A measure of training takes place in every home. In the home a child will learn trust in God or contempt for spiritual truth, responsibility or irresponsibility, honesty or dishonesty, diligence in work or indolence, and compassion or cruelty. If parents are not engaged in the task of positive, Bible-centered training, then their children will find their training in the messages offered by television, in the examples of their peers, in the influence of humanistic teachers, and in other similar ways. Let us thank God for the awesome power and influence godly parents can have over young children. Let us humbly pray for guidance in utilizing this awesome power.

NOTES

Week 22

Growing the crop of

GODLY FEAR AND REVERENCE

Some of the most admired people of our time are those who seem to laugh at fear. Race-car drivers, police officers and firefighters, astronauts and test pilots—these are among the high-risk adventurers of our day. Many fictional heroes, like those of Clive Cussler or the late Ian Fleming, also impress us with their fearlessness.

We may be tempted to think that we should be so bold, fearing nothing or no one. But there is one fear that we dare not abandon—the fear of God. It is not a cowering, haunting, paralyzing kind of dread, but a healthy and wise reverence that only the Bible can properly produce in us. Let us plant seeds of awe for the Almighty as we "garden" this week.

Plowing
Read Jeremiah 29:13.

It has been said that Christianity differs from religion in general in that Christianity emphasizes God's seeking humans and not merely humans' seeking after God. Through Jesus Christ, God has sought humans, calling us to salvation and eternal life. And yet we must not overlook the importance of our seeking after God. We are not saved through the effort and earnestness of our seeking, but by seeking we discover more of the riches of God's grace and love toward us. Let us thank God that he has first sought us and now invites us to seek him. Let us prayerfully invest our whole heart in the enterprise of seeking God.

Sowing
Read Exodus 3:1-6.

God used the burning bush to get Moses' attention. Then, when Moses was in a proper mood of reverence and quietness, he received his marching orders. We likewise need to be in an attitude of reverence when we approach the Word of God. If our minds are wandering, if we are distracted by things of the world, we will not apprehend clearly what God is saying to us. What is the burning bush God is using in an effort to gain our attention? Let us thank God for the ministry of the burning bush. Let us pray that we may be alert to whatever methods God uses to call us to reverent attention.

Cultivating
Read Joshua 5:13-15.

This is the closest thing Joshua had to a "burning bush" experience. Like Moses he turned his face from the divine visitation; like Moses, he received a command to remove his sandals because of the holy ground he stood upon; and like Moses, he was given instructions from God regarding his impending responsibilities.

What should we do when we enter the "holy ground" of public worship or personal devotions? We should remove all worldly and trivial thoughts so that we can center our attention on a holy and awesome God. Let us thank God for Joshua's example of godly fear. Let us pray that we may develop a similar reverence for God.

and our fellow human beings will be duly impressed by the God of the thunderstorm and the snowstorm.

Cultivating

Read 1 Samuel 12:16-25.

A thunderstorm may frighten us, but we understand why it thunders better than the ancient Israelites did. Nevertheless, it may be a healthy thing for us to be in awe of lightning and thunder, certainly of the God who created them. The weather in general should remind us how weak we are in the face of God's meteorological wonders. What an awesome creator God is to design these forces that defy human control! Let us thank God for these awesome aspects of weather. Let us pray that we

Watering

Read Habakkuk 2:20.

It is impossible to imagine all the earth being silent. Human voices may be heard at all hours—in our homes and on the streets, over telephones that can ring at any time, over blaring radios and in accompaniment to ever-glowing television screens. But when God speaks, everyone should be silent and listen. Let us thank God that he is always "in his holy temple," always ready for our reverent worship. Let us pray for the wisdom to be silent on those occasions when we must meditate on God's greatness and holiness.

NOTES

Week 23

Growing the crop of

GODLY MARRIAGE

It is sad to see Christian marriages ending in divorce, Christian husbands and wives becoming involved in adulterous relationships, and Christian families rocked by conflict. Certainly it is legitimate to expect Christian marriages to be more stable, stronger, and more enduring than other marriages, but it frequently is not the case. What is wrong? What attitudes and practices are missing in so many homes? What can be done to add strength, stability, and stamina to the relationships of Christian husbands and wives?

How vital it is that we sow and cultivate the good seed of God's Word into every Christian marriage! Then we can reap the harvest of happy, harmonious, God-exalting homes.

Plowing
Read 2 Corinthians 7:10, 11.

Here is a detailed description of what "godly sorrow" is all about. We should subject our efforts at repentance to the tests provided here. Are we earnest about dealing with sin and eager to clear up the matter? Is there a genuine indignation over sin's effects and a sense of alarm over the even greater damage it could have done? Do we feel a longing and a concern for other persons hurt by our sin? Are we determined to acknowledge God's justness and rightness in the matter? Let us thank God for making it clear in his Word what true repentance involves. Let us pray that he will never let us be content with a shallow, superficial kind of repentance.

Sowing
Read Ephesians 5:22-33.

It should be noted that the submission Paul urges upon the wife does not imply inferiority. It should also be observed that Paul's command to the husband involves an even more difficult responsibility. Above all, let us be reminded of the exalted nature of the marriage relationship, for it is compared here to the relationship between Christ and his church. Let us thank God for such an exalted view of marriage. Let us pray that husbands and wives will perceive the specific acts of submission and sacrifice they must make in order to bring their marriage into the center of God's will.

Cultivating
Read Proverbs 5:15-23.

It hardly needs to be said that we are living in a time of terrible temptation to sexual immorality. God has an answer to this: deep satisfaction for husband and wife through shared love, companionship, and sexual relations. If we follow God's pattern, no partner will be likely to long for sexual fulfillment outside of marriage. Let us thank God for this special way that a husband and wife can express their love and commitment to one another. Let us pray that we may not lose sight of the basic goodness and wholesomeness of sex while living in a society that distorts and abuses this gift of God.

ances. Let us also pray that husbands and wives alike may cultivate this beauty, this Christlike comeliness for each other.

Cultivating
Read 1 Peter 3:1-7.

This passage is packed with possibilities for discussion, but let us for now focus on its mention of beauty. Of course, it is inner beauty that concerns Peter. For the woman, it is "the unfading beauty of a gentle and quiet spirit." For the man, we could speak of the beauty of consideration and respect. Actually this beauty is simply a matter of applying to the marriage relationship the Christlike attitudes that we should try to develop in all our human relationships. Let us thank God for the inner beauty he gives, a beauty that transcends outward appear-

Watering
Read Hebrews 13:4.

We should not allow ourselves to think that God has relaxed his requirements regarding marriage. Unfaithfulness to marital vows is epidemic in society today, and it may be easy to assume, "that if everyone else is doing it," it must be all right. But it remains true that "God will judge the adulterer and all the sexually immoral." Let us thank God for the honor and purity he has built into the marriage relationship. Let us pray that we may do our part to preserve and promote godly marriage.

NOTES

Week 24

Growing the crop of

GRATITUDE TO OTHERS

When we watch awards shows on television, we may find it tedious to hear the award-winners thank about two dozen people for making their success possible. But how unbecoming it would be if they were to say, "I did this all by myself. I have no one to thank but myself for all my hard work, my cleverness, my persistence, and my charm." We can take some satisfaction that, although people's manners are generally in a sad state today, many persons still take time to express gratitude to others. We Christians have the help of God's Word in remembering this gracious practice. As we sow the seeds of gratitude this week, may these portions of God's Word remind us of the blessings bestowed upon us by others.

Plowing
Read Isaiah 6:1-7.

The vision of God's grandeur and holiness was sufficient to remind Isaiah of how unclean and impure he was. But our lips are just as unclean. We have soiled them with lies and gossip, cursing and obscenities, mockery and insults, and mere pointless chatter. Jesus once observed that it is what comes out of a man's mouth that makes him unclean (Matthew 15:11). We have made ourselves unclean in that way today. Let us thank God for giving us the amazing capacity for speech. But let us also pray that God will awaken us to the damage we do with our tongues and lips and help us to change our speech.

Sowing
Read 2 Samuel 9:1-13.

David had many faults, to be sure. But his devotion to God, as the Psalms illustrate, was exemplary. And his grateful devotion to his deceased friend Jonathan is a thing of beauty. David took advantage of his wealth and position to provide for Jonathan's disabled son Mephibosheth. As we have opportunity, let us demonstrate our gratitude to those who have enriched our lives. Let us offer fresh prayers of gratitude for these persons. Let us pray that we may find appropriate and edifying ways of expressing our gratitude to them personally.

Cultivating
Read Ecclesiastes 9:13-16.

He saved the city by his wisdom. But nobody remembered that poor man." In this brief story Solomon illustrates the tragedy of ingratitude. We may read it and think, "This happens to me. People forget the favors I do for them." But for our present purpose we must recall our own times of

ingratitude. How many gifts, favors, acts of kindness, and words of encouragement have we forgotten? Let us thank God for the human kindnesses we can quickly remember. Let us pray that God will bring forgotten kindnesses to mind so that we may thank both God and our human benefactors.

 ## Cultivating
Read Genesis 40:1-23.

Here is another example of a forgotten favor. The cupbearer may have thought he deserved reinstatement to Pharaoh's service. Possibly he was hesitant to jeopardize his renewed good standing with Pharaoh by speaking up for a prisoner and a foreigner. There are usually some underlying reasons for ingratitude—what are ours? Let us thank God for people who have helped us through periods of worry and fear. Let us pray that, like the chief cupbearer, we will be reminded of our shortcomings (Genesis 41:9) when we have been ungrateful.

 ## Watering
Read Romans 13:7.

What we owe some people are sincere expressions of gratitude. Who are these people? How about our parents and grandparents, preachers and teachers, neighbors and friends? We can express our appreciation face to face, by letter, or on the telephone. Perhaps a small gift would be appropriate in certain cases. Think of the good we can do in paying such debts of gratitude. Let us thank God for reminding us of those debts of gratitude to other human beings. Let us pray that he will guide us to express our gratitude in a sincere and appropriate manner.

NOTES

Week 25

Growing the crop of

HEAVENLY HOPE

According to Colossians 3:1, 2, we are to "set [our] hearts on things above, where Christ is seated at the right hand of God" and to "set [our] minds on things above, not on earthly things." We need such a reminder because we are naturally inclined toward preoccupation with earthly possessions and pleasures and with our present problems and pains. Contemplation of Heaven keeps us safe when worldly prizes threaten to lure us away from Christ. Contemplation of Heaven also encourages us when earthly defeats and disappointments shake us.

The passages we will study this week will aid us in this blessed contemplation.

Plowing
Read Acts 3:19, 20.

Are we in need of "times of refreshing"? That phrase seems to describe what we call "revival." All too often we become spiritually parched and weary through our involvement with the world and our indulgence in impure thoughts and acts. We need to be refreshed by experiencing anew the saving and sanctifying power of Jesus Christ. Repentance is the key to such refreshing. Let us thank God for the refreshment he provides for our bodies and for our spirits. Let us pray for revival and for a clearer realization of what we must do to experience revival.

 ## Sowing
Read Revelation 21:1-5.

No more bitterness of tears, tragedy of death, and ravages of pain—what a relief! We can speak of "the glorious negatives of Heaven." It will be a blessed place, in part, because of what will *not* be there. Of course, Heaven will feature many glorious positives as well, and ranking high among these will be continual access to our loving heavenly Father. Let us thank God for the prospect of sorrow's cessation, death's disappearance, and pain's permanent end. Let us pray for persistence in clinging to heavenly hope when sorrow, death, and pain afflict us on earth.

 ## Cultivating
Read Matthew 6:19-21.

How do we store up treasures in Heaven? In order to answer that, let us turn to the more obvious matter of storing up treasures on earth. We can accumulate earthly treasures such as jewelry, paintings, fine furniture, and sleek automobiles, which all represent an investment of our time and effort. To store up treasures in Heaven, we must employ that same time and effort in serving Christ and winning human souls to Heaven's King. Think about the prospect—meeting citizens of Heaven who are there because of our witness, our prayers, our teaching, and our encouragement. That is certainly more precious than any amount of jewelry or priceless paintings could be. Let us thank God that we can even now store up treasures in Heaven. Let us pray for guidance in utilizing every opportunity to gather the treasures of human souls.

Cultivating
Read 2 Corinthians 5:1-10.

Away from the body and at home with the Lord"—what assurance lies in that simple set of phrases when we stand over the casket of a beloved believer! He or she is in the presence of the Lord. When we groan over the weakness and pain afflicting our own bodies, we can be thankful that we will ultimately leave this worn-out body behind and enter the realm of the spirit to meet our Savior. Let us thank God for

the confidence that there is much more to us than a deteriorating body. Let us pray that the principle of "away from the body and at home with the Lord" will sustain us whenever we encounter death.

Watering
Read Revelation 14:13.

We will rest from our labor. Our deeds will follow us. The labor is spiritual labor; the deeds are deeds done for Christ. This verse may well be the scriptural basis for the familiar brief poem: "Only one life, 'twill soon be past./ Only what's done for Christ will last." We should throw ourselves into spiritual labor, assured that rest will soon be ours. We should dedicate ourselves to doing deeds for Christ, certain that such deeds will be remembered in eternity. Let us thank God for the fact that, although we must die, we can die in the Lord. Let us prayerfully dedicate ourselves to abundant labors for the Lord while we have time to perform them.

NOTES

Week 26

Growing the crop of

HUMILITY

I n *Poor Richard's Almanac*, Benjamin Franklin recorded his
efforts at self-improvement. One characteristic he sought to
cultivate was humility. He claimed to be so successful at
developing humility, that he was tempted to be proud of himself!
The wit of Franklin strikes a responsive chord in us. Perhaps we
too have found humility a difficult trait to master. Just when we
think we have achieved it, pride rears its ugly head again.

We should give God's Word a chance to sow in us a godly
humility, one that will consistently keep pride within its proper
limits. The Bible recognizes the deceitfulness of our pride and the
importance of a humble spirit before God. Let us plant those
seeds this week.

Plowing
Read Hosea 6:1-3.

Have you ever felt that the Lord had torn you to pieces? We speak of being "all torn up" emotionally—you may have experienced that. Or perhaps you have suffered from the actual tearing of your body or your property. We should not jump to conclusions and blame such painful experiences on the Lord. But whatever has caused the tearing, the Lord is the one who can bind up our wounds. Let us thank him for allowing even the bitter things, because they can incline our hearts toward him. Let us pray that we may turn to God as the physician who can heal our deepest hurts.

Sowing
Read Matthew 18:1-5; 19:13-15.

How is the humility of a child manifested? A child usually does not hesitate to say, "I don't know" or "I need help." A child is generally inclined to trust, to accept love, to follow guidance. As adults, we often let pride stand in the way of admitting ignorance, weakness, our longing for security, our hunger for love. Let us thank God for the illustration of humility to be found in the innocence of a child. Let us pray that we may be childlike, but not childish, in our relationships with our heavenly Father and our fellow human beings.

Cultivating
Read 1 Kings 3:4-15.

Solomon had reasons for self-confidence. He could have been haughty over the fact that, of all David's sons, he had been chosen to succeed his father. Like his own son Rehoboam later on (1 Kings 12:1-11), he could have given in to the temptation to lord it over his subjects. But Solomon humbly acknowledged his need for wisdom to rule well, and God promised him such wisdom. While we strive to build our own self-confidence, do we remember to acknowledge our dependence on God's wisdom and strength? Let us thank God for the biblical reminder that apart from him and his Son we can do nothing (John 15:5). Let us pray that we will consistently remember that and thereby be characterized by humble dependence on the Almighty.

Cultivating

Read Proverbs 11:2; 15:33; 16:18; 18:12; 29:23.

The peril of pride and the honor that comes with humility is a recurring theme in Proverbs. Excessive pride leads to disgrace and destruction. The Bible, literature outside the Bible, and current news all contain abundant examples of this truth. Why do human beings continue to allow pride to blind them and to bring them down? Why do we fail to cultivate humility? Let us thank God for pointing out to us the pitfalls of pride. Let us pray that God will bless us with humbling experiences whenever we tend to let pride overcome us.

Watering

Read Micah 6:8.

What a beautiful prospect—to walk humbly with our God! We do not walk with the swagger of self-assurance or with our eyes raised in arrogance above our fellow human beings. We walk with our head bowed in humility, with our hand trustingly clasping our Father's, and with our eyes fixed straight ahead on the path of obedience. Let us thank God for the privilege of walking humbly with him. Let us pray that we may protect that privilege through trust in and obedience to him.

NOTES

Week 27

Growing the crop of

JOY

Every Christmas we sing, "Joy to the world! the Lord is come." But we hardly live in a joyful world today, two thousand years after Jesus' first coming to earth. Conflicts across the globe rage on. Tyrants oppress their subjects. Ethnic groups continue centuries-old feuds. Many go hungry while the favored few live in extravagant displays of consumption. Indeed, joy appears to be in short supply.

Nevertheless, the potential for joy has existed since Jesus' life, death, and resurrection. It is a joy that is not altered by all of the heart-wrenching, spirit-crushing, gloom-spreading news of human woe. It is, rather, a seed we can plant, nourish, and nurture within us, and then enjoy as an ever-sustaining spiritual fruit.

Plowing
Read 2 Chronicles 7:14.

God gave this promise in response to Solomon's prayer at the dedication of the temple. Unfortunately, Solomon in later years must have forgotten this promise. He did not humble himself before God, and he did not turn from his wicked ways. But we still have a chance as individuals, as churches, and as nations to heed these words. Let us thank God for the beauty and simplicity of this Old Testament promise. Let us prayerfully give our attention to each of the steps of humbling, praying, seeking, and turning.

Sowing
Read John 16:17-24.

Complete joy, joy that no one can take away from us—that is an amazing promise. We have all known joy that was incomplete and quite temporary. An occasion of victory, success in a venture, a special time with family or friends—through these we have tasted an overflowing cup of joy, but that cup soon became empty again. Jesus never promised us an earthly existence immune to sorrow. But he surely meant for his followers to experience an underlying joy, based on his presence and promises, even in the clutches of pain and sorrow. Let us thank God for the promise of joy now and joy unending in Heaven. Let us pray for an awareness of this joy as we face life's often-bitter blows.

Cultivating
Read James 4:1-10.

What does this passage have to do with joy? It shows us the futility of looking for it in the wrong places. We are tempted to believe that joy comes through acquiring things. Or we are deluded into accepting the idea that friendship with the world and its values leads to joy. But joy is, instead, the result of submission to God, drawing near to him, resisting the devil and repenting, and humbling ourselves before the Lord. Let us thank God for the many reminders he gives us regarding the hollowness and temporal character of worldly joy. Let us pray that we may be brought into conformity with each exhortation in verses 7-10.

Cultivating
Read Galatians 5:16-26.

Joy is a part of "the fruit of the Spirit," while "the acts of the sinful nature" are destroyers of joy. Or perhaps we might say that the sinful attitudes and actions described in verses 19-21 are bitter, gnarled fruit. We have a choice as to which fruit we will grow, which fruit will make up our spiritual crop. Through prayer, meditation on the Scripture, and a conscious decision to "live by the Spirit," we can produce a crop of joy and all its kindred fruits. Let us thank God that he offers us the choice between spiritual or selfish living. Let us through prayer weed out the sinful acts listed here and grow in their place the wholesome fruit described in verses 22 and 23.

Watering
Read Romans 14:17.

The kingdom of God is a realm of joy. Heaven will be a place of indescribable joy, and we should be savoring a generous foretaste of that heavenly joy even today. If we are preoccupied with "eating and drinking," we will miss much of the joy. In this context, "eating and drinking" has reference to a critical, nitpicking attitude toward fellow Christians. Do we lose out on joy because we are focusing too much on the shortcomings of our fellow believers? Let us thank God for the kingdom of joy we have already entered. Let us pray that we will avoid spoiling that joy by looking at human foibles instead of divine glories.

NOTES

Week 28

Growing the crop of

LOVE FOR GOD

How do we envision God? Do we, like the deists of early America, see him as aloof and uninterested in our petty problems? Do we perceive him as merely a stern taskmaster and judge, bent on punishing us to the utmost limit for our sins? Or do we view him as an indulgent grandfatherly being, blithely overlooking our occasional lapses into naughtiness?

It would be difficult to *love* a God who fit into any of these categories. But the God who is revealed to us in the Bible transcends every imperfect human image of him.

As we come to appreciate more God's wisdom, might, holiness, compassion, and love for us, we will be inspired to a deeper love for him.

Plowing
Read Daniel 4:27.

This verse follows Daniel's frightening interpretation of a dream King Nebuchadnezzar had experienced in Babylon. The remainder of the chapter describes what happened when the king failed to heed Daniel's advice. We learn, however, that Nebuchadnezzar finally acknowledged that God was sovereign. Like the king, we sometimes forget that God is "Boss," and that forgetfulness inevitably leads to trouble. Let us thank God for the Bible's many reminders that he rules nature and nations. Let us pray that we may be wise enough to acknowledge at all times that God is sovereign, "that Heaven rules" (Daniel 4:26).

Sowing
Read Matthew 22:34-40.

An ancient Christian writer has given us this exhortation: "Love God, and do as you please." At first reading, that may not sound quite right. But if we sincerely love God, it will be our pleasure to do what pleases him. We need, of course, to avoid the opposite approach: "Do as you please, and then love God, so that he will forgive you." Let us thank God for our capacity for love, and for the opportunity to direct our love toward him. Let us pray that we may develop such a wholehearted love for God that we will be inspired to do only what pleases him.

Cultivating
Read Psalm 73:21-28.

What a remarkable testimony! Did not the psalmist have godly parents in Heaven? Did he not have a wife and children on earth? The answer is probably yes, but his love for God was so all-consuming that affection for human beings and for material treasures paled in comparison. This mirrors Jesus' teaching in Luke 14:25-27. There Jesus spoke of how a person's love for him must be so great as to make affection for family members seem like hatred in comparison. Let us thank God for his goodness and grace toward us, which give us abundant reasons to love him above all others. Let us pray that we may experience more of God's presence, guidance, and strengthening power so that we may love him as the psalmist did.

Cultivating

Read Psalm 84:1-12.

We may paraphrase the psalmist's sentiments in this way: "Where God has promised to be, where he is worshiped, that is where I yearn to be." Contrast this with the performance of many church members, who absent themselves from congregational worship for the most trivial reasons. Do we really love God when we have so little interest in being in the place where he is worshiped? How we need to develop the psalmist's kind of love, with its yearning for opportunities to worship God! Let us thank God that we may express our love for him through worship. Let us pray that the church we attend will conduct the kind of services that foster genuine worship.

Watering

Read Jude 21.

The topic of this section is "love for God," while Jude is speaking about God's love for us. Of course, the two are closely intertwined. In a sense, we do not have to keep ourselves in God's love, since that love for us is constant. But we do need to remind ourselves regularly of his divine love and keep ourselves responding in love to it. Let us thank God for his never-failing love for us. Let us pray that our recognition of his constant love will stir us to constant love for him.

NOTES

Week 29

Growing the crop of

MERCY

Mercy has two sides, both of which are reflected in the Scriptures we will study this week. One is God's mercy toward us, and the other is the mercy we extend to our fellow human beings.

The two cannot be separated. If we really understand and appreciate God's mercy toward us, we will be merciful to others. As we look at the greatness of the debt of which we have been forgiven, how can we legitimately withhold that same pardon from others? And as we practice mercy toward those who offend us, we will grow in our perception of the magnitude of God's mercy toward us. One could speak of a "circle of mercy." The Word of God enables us to enter into that circle.

Plowing
Read Isaiah 66:1, 2.

Here is another reminder of the overwhelming greatness of God. How puny even the strongest and cleverest of us are in comparison! How we ought to tremble at the realization of God's power and the revelation given in his Word! If we are humble and penitent and trust in him, our trembling need not be a matter of terror or dread. Let us thank God for revealing his greatness and majesty and power to us. Let us pray that we may combine our trembling at God's Word with the trust that comes through knowing his fatherly love.

Sowing
Read Romans 5:1-11.

This is a powerful passage. We need to go over it and over it to fix in our hearts and minds this glorious truth: "Christ died for the ungodly." This passage emphasizes our unworthiness—"While we were still sinners, Christ died for us"—and God's grace. Once we grasp the depth of God's grace and mercy toward us in spite of our unworthiness, we will be better able to extend mercy to all who offend us. Let us thank God anew for his abundant grace and mercy given us through Jesus Christ. Let us pray for a deeper, broader, richer understanding of this basic biblical truth.

Cultivating
Read Matthew 18:21-35.

How many times did Jesus say we should forgive another person's offenses against us? Seventy-seven times or, as the *New International Version* note has it, seventy times seven? There is quite a difference in these two figures—if the note has the correct reading, we are obligated to forgive another person 413 additional times! Of course, the point illustrated by Jesus' parable is that the abundance of the mercy we receive should compel us to extend similar forgiveness. Let us thank God for the "ten thousand talents" magnitude of his mercy toward us. Let us pray that we may perceive how small in comparison is the forgiveness we are called to grant.

Cultivating
Read Romans 12:17-21.

The idea that you could "heap burning coals on [your enemy's] head" may be appealing for the wrong reason. This does not refer to calling down a calamity upon your enemy. God would not encourage us to attempt that. On the contrary, Bible commentators point out that this expression means stirring your enemy to shame and embarrassment by treating him with kindness. This is forgiveness at its best, putting aside hopes for revenge and plotting instead how to overcome evil with good. Let us thank God for his supreme example of overcoming the evil of our sins through Christ's atoning death. Let us pray for the creative insight to see how we can overcome with good the evils done to us.

Watering
Read Matthew 5:7.

It is also biblical to say, "Blessed are those who are shown mercy, for they have a reason to be merciful." There is an inseparable relationship between divine mercy and human mercy. Of course, we do not earn God's mercy by exhibiting forgiveness toward others. Instead, our own willingness to forgive helps us appreciate God's mercy, and contemplating the grandeur of God's mercy inspires us to forgive others. Let us thank God for opportunities to be forgiving and thereby to appreciate more his mercy. Let us pray for continual growth in our understanding of God's mercy and in our own capacity for mercifulness.

NOTES

Week 30

Growing the crop of

MISSIONS-MINDEDNESS

We must never let our evangelistic vision become narrower than that of Jesus Christ. He spoke of his gospel as a message to be communicated to the whole world. Unfortunately a strange phenomenon takes place in the church today. While our newspapers and television sets keep us abreast of news from around the world, we often remain preoccupied with our own local concerns.

The passages we will read this week are designed to stir us up to missions-mindedness. When deeply planted within us, they can produce a desire for the gospel conquest of the entire earth. May we reap a great harvest of outreach as a result of these times of study.

Plowing
Read Zechariah 1:1-6.

God is speaking—are we paying attention? Of course, many people and many organizations are trying to get our attention: political candidates seeking our votes, businesses urging us to use their products or services, spokespersons for a variety of religious and philosophical viewpoints. We must be able, at times, to block out these other voices so that we can hear God's Word and respond to his bidding. Let us thank God for the power to determine to what or to whom we should give our attention. Let us pray that we may learn to "fine-tune" our attention so that God's message can come through clearly.

Sowing
Read Matthew 28:16-20.

How can we inspire all Christians to embrace the glorious cause of the Great Commission? How can we awaken every church to the magnificence of the missionary enterprise and the preciousness of personal evangelism? Certainly one way is to place ourselves prayerfully under the authority of this Great Commission. Let us thank God for the mighty challenge of our marching orders. Let us pray that we will develop an evangelistic vision to match this commission and that we will wisely undertake the practical steps involved in fulfilling that vision.

Cultivating
Read Revelation 7:9-12.

The multitude described here comes "from every nation, tribe, people and language." Imagine what it will look like, with "red and yellow, black and white" standing together there. And what a sound— God's praises being raised in English, French, Spanish, Swahili, Tagalog, and countless other tongues! And it will not be a cacophony of confusion as at the tower of Babel but a symphony of salvation songs. Let us thank God for this reminder that our heavenly home will feature a "rainbow" population. Let us pray for guidance in doing whatever we can to see that the gospel is spread among all races and nations.

Cultivating
Read Isaiah 2:1-5.

Do we want world peace? Here is how it can be achieved: by all nations hearing and responding to the teaching of God's ways. Then they will beat swords into plowshares, spears into pruning hooks, tanks into tractors, and guns into spades and hoes. Perhaps this glorious scene awaits a millennium or even the coming of the heavenly Jerusalem described in the last two chapters of Revelation. But it still gives us a gloriously bright goal for the missions enterprise. Let us thank God for the universal appeal of his truth, and especially the truth

of the gospel. Let us pray for a brighter vision of the gospel's being heard and heeded by all nations.

Watering
Read Psalm 22:27, 28.

When David, the psalmist, wrote these words about three thousand years ago, he must have marveled at this truth God's Spirit had shown him. Today we realize that the God whom David worshiped is known to people all over the earth. And yet this prophecy should stir us to reach the vast numbers who still do not know the God of David or the greater son of David, Jesus Christ. Let us thank God for the progress the gospel has already made among the nations of the world. Let us pray that more and more of earth's citizens will come to recognize that "dominion belongs to the LORD."

NOTES

Week 31

Growing the crop of

OBEDIENCE TO GOD

T he gospel song urges us to "Trust and obey, for there's no other way to be happy in Jesus, but to trust and obey." Trust, obedience, and happiness go together.

The songwriter's combination is significant. We do not really trust God if we are not willing to obey him. In the church, we place a great deal of emphasis on faith, belief, and trust, but we must not neglect the importance of obedience.

Trust is never mere assent to God's person or principles. Trust implies action.

When we believe, faith is demonstrated by compliance with the nature and norms of our Lord. The Scriptures for our study this week will aid us in giving obedience its proper emphasis.

Plowing
Read Leviticus 26:14-17.

"The wages of sin is death," according to Romans 6:23. As this passage demonstrates, the wages of sin includes a whole array of bad things. We may look at the Lord's warning here and ask, "Are sickness, blindness, defeat in battle, and the other woes here necessarily indications that we have sinned against God?" The answer is no, as the book of Job makes clear. But when we suffer, it is wise to examine ourselves and see if our suffering has a sin connection. Let us thank God for showing us throughout the Bible how sin leads to disaster. Let us pray for the insight to recognize the role sin plays in our sufferings and for the strength to forsake it.

Sowing
Read Joshua 1:1-9.

"Do not turn from it to the right or to the left." Obedience to God's Word is a straightforward, undeviating adherence to what is written. It is not a matter of thinking, "How much can I get away with and remain in God's good favor?" It does not allow us to say, "I know the Bible commands such and such, but my circumstances require a bit of leeway." What God said to Joshua, he says to all: "Be careful to obey." Let us thank God for his call to uncompromising obedience. Let us pray that we will perceive the emptiness of all our excuses for disobedience to God's Word.

Cultivating
Read 1 Samuel 15:1-23.

Like Saul, we are often tempted to obey God on our own terms. But God will settle for nothing less than full obedience to his explicit commands. Although we are under grace rather than law, God still expects obedience in such areas as marital relations, truthfulness and integrity in conducting our business, respect for human rulers and laws, and faithful worship and service in the church. We must ask, "Is our obedience in these areas in line with what God desires, or is it merely what is convenient for us?" Let us thank God for this biblical reminder of his displeasure with incomplete obedience. Let us pray for guidance in understanding what complete obedience involves and for the strength to accomplish it.

Cultivating
Read Matthew 7:21-23.

The performance of religious acts is no guarantee of salvation. Many individuals labor long in renovating a church building, preparing food for fellow church members, or serving on a church committee. Tragically, some of these religious acts are only a substitute for real obedience. Religious activity can never take the place of Christlike living, humble worship, and consistent effort at winning the lost. Let us thank God for the variety of ways in which we can work for him. Let us prayerfully make certain that our religious labors are just *part* of an overall adherence to God's ways.

Watering
Read Acts 5:29.

Sometimes obeying God requires obeying humans. Children must obey parents; citizens must obey officers of the law; church members must obey the instructions of their leaders. But when a clear choice lies before us between obedience to God and obedience to humans, we must without hesitation choose to obey God. Let us thank God for the apostles' declaration of determined obedience to God. Let us pray that we may accurately discern those situations in which obedience to God requires disobedience to humans and be faithful to God whatever the cost.

NOTES

Week 32

Growing the crop of

PATIENCE

Patience with God and patience with people are two different matters, and yet they are similar. Much of our impatience with people results from their mistakes and failures. Of course, God does not make mistakes, yet in our human weakness we are tempted to think he does. In certain circumstances—the lack of an answer to an important prayer, the experience of a tragic loss, a long delay in seeing results from diligent spiritual labors—we are inclined to question God's wisdom.

The Scriptures for this week contain references to patience in our relationship with God and with people. When we master one level of patience, we will be better able to master the other.

Plowing
Read Jeremiah 5:3.

They refused correction. . . . and refused to repent." How can we puny human beings refuse to heed the discipline of an almighty God? It is unthinkable, and we do it. The choice is clear: refuse or accept. Yet "In Acceptance Lieth Peace" is the very accurate title of a poem by Amy Carmichael. Any of us will benefit from finding it and reading it. Let us thank God for his firm but loving discipline. Let us pray that he will open our eyes to the utter foolishness of refusing to heed him.

Sowing
Read James 5:7-11.

Consider the patience of the prophets: Elijah was threatened by the evil Queen Jezebel; Jeremiah was lowered into a cistern; Daniel was thrown into a lions' den. These are only a few examples of what the Old Testament prophets endured. Have we endured anything as severe? What a challenge it is to be as patient as they were! Let us thank God for the great Old Testament accounts of God's faithful and patient prophets. Let us pray that we may benefit from their "example of patience in the face of suffering."

Cultivating
Read Psalm 37:1-11.

Wicked and worldly people *do* prosper, and sometimes we can hardly stand it! To see people who scoff at God as they revel in their wealth and pleasure is difficult to endure, but the psalmist reminds us that such a circumstance is temporary. Have patience, and soon all will be as it should be. The righteous will be blessed, and the wicked will be punished. Have patience, and keep yourself occupied with trusting in the Lord and doing good, delighting in him, and committing your way to him. Let us thank God for showing us in many places the ultimate fate of the wicked and triumph of the righteous. Let us pray for help in remembering this as we patiently persist for God in an age of mixed-up values and confusing consequences.

Cultivating
Read 1 Thessalonians 5:12-15.

Paul slips in tough little challenges every now and then. Here is a key one, "Be patient with everyone." We may say, "Thanks a lot, Paul! All you are asking us to do is to be patient with people who talk too much, people who weary us with self-pity, people who irritate us with their boasting, people who are not patient with us, and everyone else." While it seems an all-but-impossible assignment, we must declare, "With God's help I'll do it!" Let us thank God for his amazing patience with us. Let us pray that we may be inspired by his divine patience as we deal with ever-fallible human beings like ourselves.

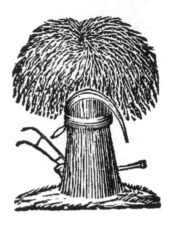

Watering
Read Psalm 40:1-3.

This is a longer passage for memorizing than most of the others in this category. But it is a very helpful one. If we will simply be patient, the Lord will hear us, lift us up, make us stand firm, and give us cause to sing. That was David's experience, and it can be ours as well. Let us thank God that he does hear the heart's cry of anyone who turns to him. Let us pray that we learn to wait patiently on his perfect timing as he responds to our cry.

NOTES

Week 33

Growing the crop of

PEACE

U niversal disarmament, equal distribution of material wealth, elimination of all religious dogma, living in harmony with our "earth mother"—people advocate a variety of approaches to initiating a reign of peace on earth.

Isaiah 11:1-9 paints a very appealing picture of peace and prophesies a time when "the earth will be full of the knowledge of the LORD as the waters cover the sea." How does such a time come about? What are the characteristics of this reign of peace? Is there a way of enjoying some elements of this utopia today?

We can utilize the riches of the Word of God to fill our hearts and minds right now with the knowledge of the God of peace and the peace of God.

Plowing
Read Isaiah 55:6, 7.

Can the Lord be found right now? Is he near? The answer to each question is yes. Because of Jesus Christ's life, death, and resurrection, we have better assurance of access to God (Romans 5:2) than the people of Isaiah's time did. But to keep the line of access open, we must forsake wicked ways and evil thoughts. Let us thank God for that blessed access to him that Christ has provided. Let us pray for the determination to forsake, abandon, and put behind us all forms of sin.

Sowing
Read John 14:1-6, 27.

What a powerful, peace-generating passage! Whenever we read it, our troubles seem to fall away, and we feel true peace—Jesus' own promised peace. Of course, many people talk about peace and offer suggestions as to how it can be achieved. But Jesus alone speaks with absolute authority. He is the way to peace; he is the truth that reveals genuine peace; he is the life that leads to perfect peace. Let us thank God for these beloved words of Jesus. Let us pray that we will develop an ever-closer friendship with the Prince of Peace.

Cultivating
Read 1 Peter 3:8-12.

We are to "seek peace and pursue it." That does not mean compromise with evil, silence about sin, or aloofness from other people's problems. Jesus was and is the Prince of Peace, and he was not guilty of such false approaches to peace. We pursue peace when we adopt the positive policy of overcoming evil with good. As long as we are mentally replaying offenses done to us and plotting some means of revenge, we will never know peace. Let us thank God for this sublime challenge of overcoming evil with good. Let us pray for the wisdom, strength, and patience to live up to the challenge.

 ## Cultivating
Read Colossians 3:5-11.

Here is an extensive list of peace-preventing attitudes and habits. Notice how decisively and drastically we are to deal with them. In one place Paul says to put these things to death. We are to slay them, execute them, annihilate them. Later Paul indicates that we should rid ourselves of these just as we would remove and fling away filthy, befouled garments. Let us thank God for these vivid ways of viewing our task of doing away with peace-preventing sins. Let us pray that we may become skilled at killing and discarding such ungodly attitudes and habits and that we may "let the peace of Christ rule in [our] hearts" (Colossians 3:15).

 ## Watering
Read Philippians 4:6, 7.

Prayer is the prescription for peace. Joseph Scriven must have cherished Paul's words, for he wrote, "O what peace we often forfeit,/ O what needless pain we bear,/ All because we do not carry/ Ev'rything to God in prayer!" What would happen if we literally brought everything before God in prayer? That would include anything that worried us or irritated us or discouraged us or tempted us. Since Paul also emphasized thanksgiving, our prayers should focus gratefully on anything that has built up our confidence, brought us joy, or strengthened us in holiness. Let us thank God for the invitation to bring everything to him in prayer. Let us pray that we will discover the key to peace through such prayer.

NOTES

Week 34

Growing the crop of

PERSONAL CONTENTMENT

Remember the LORD your God, for it is he who gives you the ability to produce wealth" (Deuteronomy 8:18). We may look at this Old Testament verse and ask, "So where is our wealth?" The truth of the matter is that, in comparison with most people of Bible times, we are wealthy.

Do we have a home filled with labor-saving appliances and reasonably nice furniture? Do we possess several changes of clothing and several pairs of shoes? Do we own at least one dependable automobile? If we can answer yes to such questions, then we should thank God for the wealth he has enabled us to obtain. And even if we seek more, we should feel a basic contentment with what we already have.

Plowing
Read Ezekiel 18:30-32.

We now know that the "new heart" and the "new spirit" are results of being born anew through Jesus Christ. But the *desire* for a new heart and spirit must come first, if we are to experience that complete rebirth. Whether unsaved or worldly Christians, these words from Ezekiel should stir us all to ask, "Are we weary enough of a heart filled with doubt, rebellion, lust, and greed to desire a profound change of heart?" Let us thank God for the power he gives to be born anew, with new hearts and new spirits. Let us pray that we will learn to cooperate with him in his plan to make us truly new creations.

Sowing
Read Philippians 4:10-20.

To be content, whatever our circumstances—can we possibly achieve that kind of attitude? If Paul could "do everything through him who gives me strength," so can we. The key is surely in recognizing that God is the supplier of our every need when we need it. Of course, we often feel that our needs require a prompter response than God seems inclined to give. But this is an area in which we must learn to yield to God's timing. Let us thank God for promising to supply all our needs. Let us pray that we will learn to be content with his timing.

Cultivating
Read Psalm 77:1-20.

Desperate prayers, sleepless nights, questioning of God's care for us—Asaph is possibly describing our own experiences. How did he regain contentment in the midst of conflict? The answer is that he remembered God's powerful actions on behalf of his people in times past. Specifically, Asaph recalled the mighty, miraculous crossing of the Red Sea in the time of Moses. We should also meditate on that event, but we have a greater deliverance than the Israelites enjoyed. We should meditate on the deliverance that came through an old rugged cross and an empty tomb. Let us thank God for the many demonstrations of his power throughout the Bible. Let us pray that we may be freshly aware of the deliverance afforded by Jesus' crucifixion and resurrection and that it will minister to us an amazing contentment.

Cultivating
Read 1 Timothy 6:6-10.

It is difficult to understand how some Christian teachers can assert that God intends for all true believers to become rich. Here Paul cautions against seeking riches, and he describes some of the dangers that a mind centered on material wealth will encounter. Let us thank

God for the "godliness with contentment" that is "great gain." Let us pray for an attitude toward material things that avoids the perils of "wanting to get rich," "the love of money," or being "eager for money."

Watering
Read Hebrews 13:5.

Be content with what you have." How do we apply that? Is it wrong for us to desire a larger home, a more dependable car, a higher standard of living? Surely the point here is that we must avoid fretting over money and focusing too much of our attention on material things. It is possible to find satisfaction with our present economic status while at the same time seeking improvement. We simply need to keep our priorities in their proper order. Let us thank God abundantly for what we presently possess. Let us pray that, as we seek reasonable improvement in our finances, we will not lose sight of our trust in him and our contentment in his care.

NOTES

Week 35

Growing the crop of

PERSONAL DISCIPLINE

We live in what may be called "the era of waste." While recreation is a legitimate aim for refreshing body and mind, our society wastes far too much time, money, and energy on various recreational pursuits.

Our hectic lifestyles also contribute to a good deal of material waste. We are caught up in a "use-and-throw-away" mentality. Much of this waste could be avoided if we were to practice personal discipline.

The Christian is particularly obligated to cultivate discipline in the use of time, money, and energy, because the New Testament in many places commands it. Let us plant a few of these passages in our hearts.

Plowing
Read 1 Samuel 7:2-4.

Mourning over sin is a good beginning, but it is only the beginning. The people of Israel had been mourning their sins, but Samuel told them they needed to take the further step of ridding themselves of false gods. We mourn over the mess our sins have put us in, the effect they have on people we love, or the barrier they place between us and God. But what kind of action do we take to rid ourselves of every trace of the sin? Let us thank God for giving us the capacity to mourn over our sins. Let us also pray for a "Samuel" who will stir us to action against sin.

Sowing
Read 2 Timothy 2:1-7.

The soldier, the athlete, and the farmer—they are all examples of discipline. We will focus on the athlete in the next three Scriptures, so for the moment let us think of the soldier, training body and mind in order to perform his duty. Let us think of the farmer, carefully expending time and energy to raise his crop. We have our duty to perform, and we have a spiritual harvest to reap—let us submit ourselves to the discipline these require. Let us thank God for the illustrations provided by the soldier and the farmer regarding our need for spiritual discipline. Let us pray that we may indeed "reflect on what [Paul is] saying" and that the Lord will give us insight into his call for discipline.

Cultivating
Read 1 Corinthians 9:24-27.

If you are a Christian, you are a long-distance runner and a boxer, whether or not you like it. So you had better whip yourself into peak condition for your athletic endeavors. This is a race and a contest in which it is true that "winning is everything." What a tremendous reminder we have here of the importance of physical, mental and spiritual discipline in living the Christian life! Let us thank God for the "crown that will last forever," which spurs us on to a disciplined and determined race. Let us pray for guidance in developing the "strict training" that will make us victorious runners.

Cultivating
Read Philippians 3:12-21.

An athlete cannot afford to look back. Successes or failures from the past must not affect his or her present performance. And Christians cannot linger too long over past victories or wallow in the guilt of old sins. "Forgetting what is behind and straining toward what is ahead," we must press on heavenward. And knowing that "our citizenship is in heaven" should help us do that. Let us thank God that we can put the past behind

us. Let us pray for the concentration we need to keep our spiritual sight focused on Heaven, our home.

Watering
Read Hebrews 12:1, 2.

Jesus is the perfect example of discipline for the spiritual athlete. He "endured the cross," fulfilling his mission and refusing to let the shamefulness of the cross be a hindrance to him. We have our mission, and we face an array of hindrances in the way of our completing it. But if we rely on the kind of discipline Jesus exemplifies, we can fulfill it. Let us thank God for Jesus' example of determined effort. Let us pray for the discernment to recognize our hindrances and entanglements and for the determination to overcome them.

NOTES

Week 36

Growing the crop of
PERSONAL HOLINESS

T he hymn writer urges us to "Take time to be holy." It does take significant time to sow and cultivate God's kind of holiness. As the poet notes, such holiness grows only when communication with God is rich and full.

That is a benefit of this approach to Bible study. Here we come to a place in our spiritual field or garden that we might be inclined to pass over. There are much more pleasant crops to grow: love, joy, peace, heavenly hope, and the like. But holiness calls for an often-painful separation from habits and attitudes that have become deeply rooted within us. Nevertheless, we dare not neglect the exhortation—"Take time to be holy!"

Plowing
Read Amos 5:4-6.

Bethel, Gilgal, and Beersheba were cities in which polluted worship was offered to God, worship that was of human origin. God has set forth in the Bible the standards by which he wants to be worshiped and served. If we are to seek him and live, we must pay heed to his standards. Let us thank God for demonstrating clearly in his Word the kind of worship and service he requires. Then let us pray for the diligence to seek out and adhere to his standards.

Sowing
Read 1 Peter 1:13-16.

Are Christians any different from others? Or do they fall prey to the same temptations, think the same wicked thoughts, and perform the same evil deeds? We must be different, for we are called to imitate the holiness of God: "Be holy, because I am holy." Let us thank God that he has made us new creations with the potential to live new, more godly lives. Let us pray that we will be aware of the areas of our lives that still need changing and that we will grow in the courage and strength needed to make the changes.

Cultivating
Read Romans 6:11-14.

Here is a way of viewing our bodies and their various parts. Our hands are God's instruments, dedicated to serving him and not some unholy cause. Our feet are his, for taking us where he leads and not to some place where immorality reigns. Our tongues are also his, and we are obligated to use them for promoting righteousness rather than evil. Our eyes are meant to view what is pure and wholesome (although our service for Christ may sometimes bring us into surroundings where sin's influence is visible) and not to be consciously focused on smutty literature or immoral movies. Let us thank God for our marvelous bodies, with their versatile array of individual parts. Let us pray that we may constantly dedicate our bodies to actions and habits that will bring him glory.

Cultivating
Read Hebrews 12:14-17.

Without holiness no one will see the Lord." What a sobering reminder that is! Church attendance, or even service in the church, is no guarantee of experiencing the grace of God, if we fail to practice purity. Let us thank God for his call to holiness and for providing in the Bible clear guidelines to a holy life. Let us pray that God will open our eyes to the importance of cultivating holiness and that we will conform to his standards of holiness.

Watering
Read Philippians 4:8.

If Paul had been writing in the computer age, he might have said, "Program your minds according to what is true, noble, and right." We do not have room here for an extensive comparison between a computer and the human mind, but one important parallel lies in the control the programmer or user possesses. We have the power to determine the input our mental computer will receive. If we put in the good things Paul lists, then the output will be holy habits and deeds. Let us thank God for the lessons we can draw regarding our minds in this computer age. Let us pray for a clearer realization of the marvel of our minds and for a more rigorous control over what goes into them.

NOTES

Week 37

Growing the crop of

PRAYERFULNESS

If it is a natural act to pray, then it seems that great numbers of people today are living unnaturally. Even those who occasionally resort to prayer may operate on the philosophy that says, "The small things I can handle all by myself. The big things require a little help from God."

According to the Bible, we need to exercise prayer at all times and under all circumstances. No situation we face is too insignificant or trivial for the interest of the caring Father. Likewise, no challenge is greater than the strength of our powerful Father.

Certainly any Christian should aim at being an accomplished practitioner of prayer. The following Scriptures represent a valuable starting point in achieving such an aim.

Plowing
Read Daniel 9:3-6.

Is pleading a part of prayer? We tend to think of pleading as a tactic people use to try to change God's mind. As a man of God, Daniel would not have dared to imagine he could change God's mind, yet he pleaded in prayer. Perhaps this merely indicates an emotional involvement in prayer. If our prayers are inclined to be rather formal, matter-of-fact speeches to God, we may need to do some pleading ourselves. Let us thank God that in prayer we can approach him in honesty; we can be ourselves. Let us pray for an emotional involvement in prayer, confessing our sins and crying out for greater victory over temptation.

Sowing
Read Luke 11:1-13.

What is the most important request a Christian can make for himself or herself in prayer? According to this passage, the answer would be "the Holy Spirit." Of course the Holy Spirit dwells in us once we become Christians. The point of praying for the Holy Spirit is that we want him to be more in control of us, to guide us and strengthen us, and to bring forth in us his abundant fruit (Galatians 5:22, 23). Let us thank God for the privilege of praying for his Spirit's ministry in us. Let us pray that we will become fit vessels for the Holy Spirit, and that he will work mightily in us and through us.

Cultivating
Read Daniel 6:1-10.

If our society had a law against praying to God, would we be in danger of prosecution? Or, to put it in a form more applicable to our circumstances, do we give prayer the priority that Daniel did? Prosecution is unlikely to be a problem for our prayer lives, but lack of perseverance may be. We have an enemy, the devil, who opposes our prayers by whispering to us, "Prayer is a waste of time! It takes too much effort! God is not listening!" We must answer, "I believe in prayer because I believe in a God who hears and answers prayer! I am determined to keep on praying!" Let us thank God for Daniel's example of perseverance in prayer. Let us pray for the determination to resist the devil's efforts to halt our prayer lives.

Cultivating
Read Luke 6:12-16.

The natural inference of this passage is that Jesus spent all night in prayer seeking guidance from the Father as preparation for choosing his twelve apostles. Does our dependence on prayer when *we* must make important decisions measure up to this standard? Jesus meant to lay before us a perfect example. And if we are to follow his example of prayerfulness, we must probably pray much more often than we do at present. Let us thank God for the Gospels' revelation of Jesus as a man of prayer. (Among other references in Luke that demonstrate this are 3:21; 5:16; 9:18, 28; 11:1.) Let us pray that we will reach an understanding as to how much God wants us to pray and that we will fulfill his wishes.

Watering
Read Psalm 55:17.

Hopefully we do not often need to cry out in distress to God. But to pray to him at evening, morning, and noon is still a good policy. In the Hebrew way of thinking, the new day began in the evening. For us, prayer at bedtime as we contemplate the coming day can be very helpful. Morning prayer as we prepare to face our daily responsibilities is another good step. Prayer at noon can help us deal with problems that have a risen and can fortify us for the remainder of the day. Let us thank God that we can pray to him at any time. Let us pray for the wisdom to schedule seasons of frequent prayer.

NOTES

Week 38

Growing the crop of

PRAYING WHEN AFFLICTED

The previous crop centered our attention on prayer in general. Here we focus specifically on prayer in affliction. In so doing, we acknowledge that human beings sometimes seem to forget prayer when trouble comes. Why is this? Why do we tend to turn away from God when we need him most?

Perhaps we are disappointed in God for allowing the suffering in the first place. Perhaps we are inclined to say, "I can handle this all by myself." Perhaps the crisis is so sudden or so severe that it causes us temporarily to overlook the fact that we have a Father who cares.

We need to sow the following Scriptures to help us make the proper, prompt, prayerful response at the onset of any affliction.

Plowing
Read Job 42:1-6.

Job told God, "I despise myself and repent in dust and ashes." Are we also supposed to despise ourselves? We are certainly to despise some of the words we speak and some of the deeds we do. It is good to despise our tendencies to excessive pride and selfish grasping of material things. But some people engage in the kind of self-loathing that leads them to regard themselves as beyond even divine help. That is not what is meant here. Let us thank God that in his sight we have great value, a value that caused him to give his Son for us. Let us pray that we will learn to despise and remove from us those attitudes and habits that displease our gracious Father.

Sowing
Read Psalm 34:1-7.

What do we normally do when affliction comes? Feel sorry for ourselves? Complain to God and to other people? Stiffen our backs and try to endure it? The best response is to pray as David did. He makes it sound so simple: "I sought the LORD . . . he delivered me." "This poor man called, and the LORD . . . saved him." The deliverance may not have come immediately. It is likely that David had to pray persistently until at last he had his answer. It should work that way for us too, and it can if we will only pray persistently. Let us thank God that he is aware of our afflictions and cares about our crises. Let us pray that we will develop the prayer habit as a first and persistent response to any trial.

Cultivating
Read Luke 18:1-8.

Three of the easiest words to utter are, "I give up." But Jesus' desire is that we "always pray and not give up." We must pray faithfully, fervently, persistently, and with determination. Jesus' parable indicates that it may require a substantial measure of persistence to gain victory over affliction. But he gives us an assurance that such persistence pays off. Let us thank God for his many reminders regarding persistence in prayer. Let us pray that we may become true prayer warriors, waging war on our knees to gain victories for others and for ourselves.

Cultivating
Read James 5:13-18.

"The prayer of a righteous man is powerful and effective." Consider the challenge laid before us by this statement. We must cultivate righteousness, and we must pray "in faith" (v. 15) and "earnestly" (v. 17). That will enable us to achieve a prayer life that is truly powerful, a dynamic prayer life like that of Elijah. Then we can transform afflictions into advances and trials into triumphs. Let us thank God for the powerful potential of prayer. Let us pray that we may become potent practitioners of prayer.

Watering
Read 1 Thessalonians 5:17.

How do we "pray continually" or "pray without ceasing," as the *King James Version* translates this verse? Our minds and lips are occupied with doing our jobs, interacting with our families and friends, and enjoying a legitimate amount of recreation. Right now, of course, we are focusing on prayer as a response to affliction. When we are hurting or facing a crisis, it is often easier to find opportunities to pray. But we need to make continual prayer a habit so that when difficult times arise it will be natural for us to resort to prayer. Let us thank God that he is always listening to our prayers. Let us pray that we may learn the skill of continual prayer, both in times of affliction and at all other times.

NOTES

Week 39

Growing the crop of

REJOICING

This is the day the LORD has made; let us rejoice and be glad in it" (Psalm 118:24). Every day is a day the Lord has made: the day of triumph and the day of defeat, the day of success and the day of disappointment, the day of reunion and the day of parting again. We must rejoice in every God-given day, realizing that the Giver is both wise and good and that the flow of pleasant and painful earthly days will soon give way to the eternal day of triumph, success, and glad reunion.

Of course, this is very much against our selfish nature. We flinch at pain, pout at disappointment, and groan at drudgery. Our time in the Word this week will help us celebrate when our carnality prompts us to mourn.

Plowing
Read Ezra 10:1-4.

Thanks to Ezra's leadership, the Israelites were penitent about having married heathen wives. And they were ready to take action to remedy this wrongdoing. What kinds of evil, immoral relationships are threatening our obedience to God? What steps do we need to take to avert this danger? Let us thank God that he warns us in Scripture of the danger of unwholesome and unspiritual relationships. Let us pray for the courage to terminate any relationships that threaten our commitment to Jesus Christ.

Sowing
Read 1 Peter 4:12-19.

Rejoicing is not so much a matter of emotion as it is of the will. That is, Christians do not rejoice because they feel good or because everything is going well for them. Instead, they rejoice in spite of pains and trials because God commands them to rejoice. Of course, we do not rejoice unreasonably, for we know that all our sufferings will ultimately be swallowed up in the victory Christ has won and is even now winning. Let us thank God that we are privileged to suffer in the way Christ suffered. Let us pray that we may perceive more clearly the ultimate victory that gives us cause for continual rejoicing.

Cultivating
Read Acts 5:40-42.

Rejoicing because of what? See what it says: "The apostles . . . [were] rejoicing because they had been counted worthy of suffering disgrace for the Name." Can you imagine how dumbfounded the Sanhedrin must have been? They had flogged the apostles and warned them to be silent about Jesus. But those twelve men were smiling, singing, celebrating as they went out and resumed their usual preaching. Is this the reason we are told soon afterward that "a large number of priests became obedient to the faith" (Acts 6:7)? Let us thank God for this amazing ability of the apostles to rejoice in suffering for Christ. Let us pray that we may imitate the apostles in this way.

Cultivating
Read Acts 16:22-34.

A gospel concert in prison —what a scene! What are some hymns *we* can sing in the midst of suffering? How about "A Mighty Fortress Is Our God," "Blessed Assurance," "Sweet Will of God," "My Jesus, I Love Thee"? These are only a few examples. Perhaps by our rejoicing in song we will generate a kind of spiritual earthquake and lead people to say, "What must we do to be saved?" Let us thank God for the abundance of hymns we possess that help us express faith and devotion. Let us pray that we may learn to keep a spiritual song in our hearts, if not on our lips, at all times.

Watering
Read 1 Thessalonians 5:16.

T his verse is not too difficult to memorize. You can probably handle both the *King James Version* ("Rejoice evermore.") and the *New International Version* ("Be joyful always.") at the same time. This exhortation would seem to be a case of "whistling past the graveyard," if it were not in the New Testament context of a sin-conquering, death-defeating, crucified and risen Christ. Because we know him, we have cause for rejoicing whatever our circumstances. Let us thank God for the mighty challenge contained in this brief verse. Let us pray that we will never lose sight of our reason for rejoicing.

NOTES

Week 40

Growing the crop of

RESTFULNESS IN SLEEP

Christians should sleep better than any other people. After all, we accept the principles of God's control over his creation and of his constant care for us. If we identify with the children's prayer and its concern that we might die before we wake, we have confidence that the Lord "our soul will take."

We should enjoy restful, refreshing sleep, but do we? Do we retire confidently at the end of the day, or are our nights consumed with worry and regret? Is our sleep sound, or does the turmoil of the day continue to echo in our minds, resulting in sleepless agitation? What can we do to rest soundly in the arms of God?

The following Scriptures, planted within us, may help us reap nights of more satisfying slumber.

Plowing
Read Zephaniah 2:3.

To be sheltered from the Lord's anger—that is an aim we can appreciate. We have perhaps trembled in times past because of the wrath of parents, teachers, employers, and other authority figures. But to face the anger of the Almighty is an almost unimaginable prospect. Let us humbly seek him now and find that perfect shelter from his anger. Let us thank God for our ultimate shelter from God's wrath: the reconciliation we have gained through Jesus Christ. Let us pray that we may not be so foolish as to seek any other shelter.

Sowing
Read Psalm 3:1-8.

Every night we lock our doors and windows. Perhaps we have installed an alarm system or merely rely on an alert family dog. In one way or another, we all protect ourselves and our property while we are asleep. But here the psalmist speaks of our ultimate protection—the Lord shields us and sustains us. Let us thank God for the awareness that he watches over us while we sleep. Let us pray for a clear realization of the fact that God is watching over us when we sleep *and* when we are awake.

Cultivating
Read Proverbs 3:21-26.

What are the characteristics of sweet sleep? It certainly involves our promptly falling asleep and not lying awake with our worries. Sweet sleep is surely free of disturbing nightmares, and it is the kind of sleep from which we awaken in the morning refreshed and ready for a new day. Solomon tells us that giving priority to sound judgment and discernment from God will enable us to enjoy such sweet sleep. Let us thank God for his many promises of blessings on those who seek him through his Word. Let us pray for the wisdom to put our confidence in God both day and night so that earthly worries may not ruin our rest.

Cultivating
Read Mark 4:35-41.

Here we see two remarkable things: Jesus sleeping in the storm and Jesus speaking to the storm. The first could make us envious. How was Jesus able to sleep with the boat rolling on the waves, the spray slowly soaking him, his disciples struggling to keep the boat from sinking? We lose sleep over such smaller things as unpaid bills, an approaching dentist's appointment, or an upcoming difficult job. When Jesus lay down, he must have spoken to himself the same command he later gave the storm: "Quiet! Be still!" Oh, that he would speak these words to us in our sleepless nights! Let us thank God for Jesus' remarkable example of sleep in the midst of a storm. Let us pray that his awesome com-

mand, "Quiet! Be still!" may sound out from the pages of Scripture to calm our restless souls.

Watering
Read Psalm 4:8.

How many people can really "lie down and sleep in peace"? How many lie awake worrying about tomorrow instead? How many toss and turn, agitated by what has happened during the day? This beautiful verse seems to be a kind of spiritual sedative. If we can let it permeate our minds, it will do us more good than anything we might purchase at the drugstore. Let us thank God for the promise of peaceful sleep. Let us pray that we may develop the psalmist's assurance of such sleep and experience it each time we lie down.

NOTES

Week 41

Growing the crop of

RESTING IN THE LORD

Managing stress is a recurring theme of books, public addresses, television talk-show segments, and magazine articles. The popularity of that theme results from our having stressful jobs, stressful homes, and, in too many cases, stressful churches.

It is no overstatement to say that the Bible offers the greatest array of stress-relievers available. But there is nothing magical about the words of Scripture. They work only when received with an attitude of trust toward their divine Giver.

The following passages call us to such trust and to its resulting rest. May we learn to take shelter in the Lord this week. He alone can truly handle our stress.

Plowing
Read Deuteronomy 4:29.

God does not play "hide-and-seek" with us. We are to seek him, but not because he is hiding. It would be more accurate to say that *we* are hiding from him. Like Adam and Eve in the garden (Genesis 3:8-10), we hide because we are sinners, and we fear being in the presence of a holy God. But God wants us to seek him and find him so that we may benefit from his boundless mercy and share a loving fellowship with him. Let us thank God for his blessed invitation to seek him. Let us pray that we will abandon our hiding places and enter into the presence of our gracious God.

Sowing
Read Psalm 116:1-7.

Be at rest once more, O my soul, for the LORD has been good to you." That bears repeating over and over again. It is not a matter of self-delusion, for the Lord *has* been good to us. He has provided us a way of salvation, guided us through confusing times, comforted us when we were hurting, and healed us when we were sick. And he will continue to be good to us. We have excellent reasons for enjoying a profound sense of rest in our innermost beings. Let us thank God for the many ways in which he has been good to us. Let us pray that we will eliminate any tendencies to question his goodness.

Cultivating
Read Psalm 23:1-6.

Have you seen any sheep lately? Even better, have you seen any sheep guided by a shepherd? You probably haven't, yet the scenes depicted in this psalm speak to all of us. We can identify with lying down in the green pastures, walking near the quiet waters, and walking through the valley of the shadow of death. We can appreciate the shepherd's provision, guidance, and comfort. Consequently, people everywhere find rest in hearing or reading this beloved psalm. Let us thank God for this Psalm and for those occasions when it has ministered to us. Let us pray for a deeper appreciation of God's shepherd care for us.

Cultivating
Read Isaiah 4:2-6.

The Lord will provide "a shelter and shade from the heat of day, and a refuge and hiding place from the storm and rain." This is symbolic language with which we can identify. How many times has our rest been hindered by oppressive heat or by a house-rattling thunderstorm? Or, to go behind the symbols, how many times has the heat of trials or the storms of temptation made us restless? The Lord is the perfect giver of rest—let us thank him for that. Let us also pray that we will learn to rest in him in the face of external and internal storms.

Watering
Isaiah 26:3, 4.

A mind centered on God, attuned to trusting God, will surely be at rest. Of course, we will inevitably encounter the restlessness of a world alienated from God, the turbulence of human beings in conflict with one another. Further, we should not try to avoid this, because we are here to serve the suffering ones and to give hope to those harassed by evil. But we should regularly return our thoughts to God and renew our sense of rest in him as "the Rock eternal." Let us thank God that we may center our minds on him. Let us pray that we may not only rejoice in the rest God provides us but also share it with others who are restless.

NOTES

Week 42

Growing the crop of

REVIVAL IN THE CHURCH

A familiar prayer features the plea: "Lord, revive Your church, beginning with me." If the church we attend has become lifeless and stagnant, we should regard ourselves as the key to igniting revival. It is futile to waste our energy blaming the minister, church leaders, elders, or anyone else for the church's sad state.

It is fruitful, however, to humble ourselves before God, practice thorough repentance, fill our hearts with God's Word, and pray fervently that revival may begin with us. The Scriptures below can be a good starting point for such a crusade. Darkness cannot swallow the light of a single match. When we sow the seeds of personal revival, can community awakening be far behind?

Plowing
Read Romans 2:5-11.

Stubbornness is one of those qualities that can be good or bad. Paul does not use the word in verse 7, but we could substitute it for "persistence" when we read Paul's statement, "To those who by persistence in doing good seek glory, honor and immortality, he will give eternal life." When stubbornness involves persistence in doing evil and in resisting God's call to repentance, it is unspeakably bad. Let us thank God for his call to persistence in doing good. Let us pray for an awareness of any stubborn resistance we may harbor against God's will and for the strength to yield it up.

Sowing
Read Ephesians 1:15-23.

Here is a prayer that we can profitably utilize on behalf of our own churches. The word "revival" may not appear here, but if these mighty prayer aims are fulfilled in our congregation, we will definitely experience revival, renewal, and revitalization. Paul's prayer focuses on the resurrection of Jesus Christ (verse 20) and on the fact that he is the head of the church, his body (verses 22, 23). Let us thank God that as the body of Christ we have a constant connection with our head—the crucified and resurrected Christ. Let us pray that we will be ever more responsive to our head and thereby experience revival through him.

Cultivating
Read Acts 19:13-20.

No responsible person today would publicly advocate burning books. But what happened at Ephesus surely applies to us. When the believers did away with what was sinful and Satanic in their lives, revival came. Do we have books and magazines in our homes that we should quietly dispose of? Do we practice ungodly habits and harbor unspiritual attitudes of which we should repent? Concrete acts of repentance can clear the way to revival in our congregations. Let us thank God for the challenge of eliminating from our lives anything that can block his Spirit's power from working in us. Then let us prayerfully and boldly accept his challenge.

Cultivating
Read Acts 4:23-37.

Prayer brought revival, and what a revival it was! The church in Jerusalem exhibited an amazing unity, an unquenchable enthusiasm for evangelism, and a remarkable spirit of giving. The prayer that led to this revival can be summarized as follows: "Lord, help us, in spite of what others may say or do, to accomplish what will glorify you and your Son Jesus." What would happen if we consistently prayed that kind of prayer for our churches? Let us thank God for the power of prayer in promoting revival. Let us pray for a soul-shaking revival like that of the Jerusalem church.

Watering
Read Psalm 85:6.

This verse lies behind the gospel song, "Revive Us Again." It is an excellent prayer, both in the verse and in the song. But do we really want to be revived? If we were to experience revival, we would turn our zeal away from pleasures and possessions and direct it into our worship of God and our service for God. We would have to give up our habit of groaning and criticizing and do some first-rate rejoicing. Let us thank God for his willingness to revive us. Let us pray that we will get serious about revival and about doing what we must do to prepare for it.

NOTES

Week 43

Growing the crop of

SEXUAL PURITY

Sexual purity was difficult to maintain in biblical times because various heathen religions practiced a kind of sacred prostitution. It was a religious act to give one's body to priests and priestesses within many pagan temples. Today, sexual purity is equally difficult to maintain. Temptations to illicit desire are everywhere. Movies, television programs, popular music, books and magazines seem to unite in a chorus of "Don't wait—do it!" The amoral behavior of various politicians, entertainers, sports heroes, and other supposed role models reinforces the idea that chastity is passé, virginity is undesirable, and monogamy is stifling. How we need the clear voice of Scripture, pointing us to sexual purity!

Plowing
Read Malachi 3:6, 7.

"How are we to return?" Is that question an obstinate response to the Lord's call? Or were the people sincere in their perplexity as to how they could repent and turn their lives around? Whatever the answer may be, we have no cause in this Christian era for obstinacy or perplexity. Jesus Christ, through his death and resurrection, has opened up the way of return to God. What we must do is to trust in Jesus, follow him, and be obedient to his commands. Let us thank God for the clarity of the gospel message and of what we must do to respond to it. Let us pray that we will allow nothing to cloud the clear truth of the gospel.

Sowing
Read Job 31:1-12.

What a wise policy—to make a covenant with our eyes! We can say, "Eyes, I will allow you to gaze upon the beauty of blue skies, green meadows, and multicolored flowers. I will permit you to focus on the innocent faces of young children, the smiles of senior saints, and the earnest expressions on the countenances of those who worship the Lord. But I will not permit you to linger on any scene that would incite me to impure thoughts." Let us thank God for the power we have to control what our eyes will look upon. Let us pray for the wisdom to work out our own personal covenants with our eyes.

Cultivating
Read Matthew 5:27-30.

Should we be seeing more one-eyed, one-handed people? Given the fact that there is obviously a good deal of lust being entertained in human minds—and taking Jesus' words quite literally—the answer would have to be yes. It is clear, however, that Jesus was speaking figuratively here. Since lust resides in the heart and mind, removing an eye or a hand would not affect it. But Jesus was advocating a drastic dealing with lust. What might this involve? Some possibilities are breaking a questionable friendship, altering one's television viewing habits, and discontinuing the reading of certain magazines or books. Let us thank God for demonstrating the dangers of an undisciplined sex drive. Let us pray for the insight as to what "eyes" and "hands," what sources of sexual temptation, we may need to cut off.

Cultivating
Read 1 Thessalonians 4:1-8.

We can learn to control our own bodies! Perhaps that is true only of Christians, but it is likely true of human beings in general. Too often "experts" suggest that the sex drive is so strong as to be uncontrollable. But we have the power to say no to illicit, destructive sexual relationships. And, of course, we can say yes to the pure sharing of God's gift of sex within the context of marriage. Let us thank God for the power of choice he gives regarding the satisfaction of physical appetites. Let us pray that we may boldly challenge others to control their sexual appetites.

Watering
Read Matthew 5:8.

How pure is pure? An old soap commercial spoke of a product that was 99.44 percent pure. We, on the other hand, must aim for perfect purity. If we slip and allow an impure thought to dwell in our mind or fall prey to the temptation to engage in an immoral act, then we must start over again to aim for perfect purity. Let us thank God for the glorious prospect of seeing him in Heaven. Let us pray that we may begin immediately the habit of focusing our thoughts only on what is pure, righteous, and godly.

NOTES

Week 44

Growing the crop of
SPIRITUAL POWER

The desire for power usually seems to be a selfish aim. A person seeks financial power so that he or she can acquire more things and attain "the good life." Various groups clamor for political power because they want greater influence in shaping society according to their values. Even candidates for public office, who declare their wish to be "public servants," often impress us as hungering for the media attention and the many perquisites that come with the job.

If we long for spiritual power, it must be because we genuinely desire to render better service to God and our fellow human beings. May that desire and that motive be the results of our study this week.

Plowing
Read Psalm 51:16, 17.

How can we ask God to give us "a broken and contrite heart"? Who wants a broken heart or a broken spirit? Yet the Bible indicates that brokenness is the way to blessing, that a hurting heart can lead to healing. We have to accept the fact that we are not all right the way we are. Even if we are long-time Christians, worldly attitudes and values tend to keep a grip on us. It takes a measure of brokenness to overcome these. Let us thank God that he allows hearts to be broken so that he can heal them. Let us pray that we will not shrink from brokenness, but welcome it as a tool of grace.

Sowing
Read Ephesians 3:14-21.

Notice that three times in this passage Paul prayed that his readers might have power. Notice also that we are among those readers! It hardly needs to be emphasized that Paul was not speaking of military, economic, political, or physical power. He prayed for "power through [God's] Spirit in your inner being." Contrary to what some Christian leaders say, this is the power we should seek. Let us thank God that he "is able to do immeasurably more than all we ask or imagine." Let us pray that we may obtain and utilize that power for God's "glory in the church and in Christ Jesus."

Cultivating
Read 2 Corinthians 12:7-10.

God's strength is made perfect in weakness. That is difficult to comprehend. All too often, we feel that we need to be strong of mind and body to serve the Lord most effectively. In addition, self-assurance and self-assertiveness are highly valued in our society. But it is easy to place too much confidence in the keenness of our mental powers or the impressiveness of our physical appearance. Let us thank God that his strength is made perfect in our weaknesses. Let us pray that we will be made aware of our weaknesses and of our need for God's grace and power.

means for us to have and use. Let us pray for his guidance in growing this faith that is "as small as a mustard seed."

Cultivating

Read Matthew 17:14-21.

What are some mountains we ought to be moving? Unless we work for mining companies or road crews, we have little need for moving literal mountains of earth and rock. But Jesus was referring here to lofty challenges such as overcoming temptations, conquering spiritual enemies, winning the lost, and building the church. Jesus demonstrated his power by healing the demon-possessed boy, and he offers us the power through faith to work mighty works today. Let us thank God for this vivid illustration of the power Jesus

Watering

Read 2 Timothy 1:7.

How does timidity hurt us? Does it keep us from sharing our faith with friends and acquaintances? Is it a barrier to accepting a place of service in our churches? Does it stand in the way of our voicing a firm "No!" to temptations non-Christians place before us? We have good news here! The spirit of timidity can give way to a spirit of power! Let us thank God that he can give us power to overcome weakness, hesitancy, and timidity in speaking up for him. Let us also prayerfully open our hearts to that gift of power.

NOTES

Week 45

Growing the crop of

SPIRITUAL WISDOM

It has been observed that common sense is not so common as the term implies. Instead, every day we see various examples of human foolishness, shortsightedness, and outright stupidity. Indeed, if the human race were dependent only on common sense for survival, we would soon self-destruct.

That is what appears to be happening in our time, as more and more people reject God's eternal wisdom. Like those who lived in the time of the judges, people seek to do what is right in their own eyes. (See Judges 21:25, *King James Version*.) How we Christians need to sow and cultivate spiritual wisdom, so we can rise above the common sense of our day! Seek that guidance in the Word this week.

Plowing
Read Isaiah 57:15.

We human beings tend to be quite proud of ourselves. Look what we've done: sent men and machinery into space, designed intricate computers, constructed mammoth sports stadiums, created a vast network of communications systems, and the like. But in spite of all this, we must be "lowly in spirit" to enjoy fellowship with God. Let us thank God that he has given us such abilities and skills. But let us also pray that we will not let pride in human accomplishments and in our own personal achievements blind us to our need for lowliness before the Almighty.

Sowing
Read 1 Corinthians 1:18-31.

Now, as in Paul's time, there are many people who view the message of the cross as weak and foolish. We may encounter some of these in our neighborhoods and in our places of work. If not, we can easily find their viewpoint expressed in the media. This dramatic passage meets that kind of human ignorance head on. In ringing words Paul declares that the preaching of Christ crucified is "the power of God and the wisdom of God." Let us thank God for the wisdom that is centered in the cross of Christ. Let us pray that we will so embrace this wisdom that the world's opposition will not shake us.

Cultivating
Read 1 Corinthians 2:1-10.

Paul was referring to his own time when he spoke of "the wisdom of this age or of the rulers of this age." But it is still true that popular wisdom often stands in contrast to the wisdom of God. Then, as now, the popular wisdom exalts military power and material plenty over spiritual realities. It is more concerned with satisfying physical appetites than it is with assuaging the hunger of the soul. Let us thank God for his wisdom that exceeds the reach of human eyes, ears, and minds. Let us pray that we will be discerning in our dealings with the popular wisdom and not let it influence us when it opposes the wisdom of God.

Cultivating

Read James 3:13-18.

The devil has his own brand of wisdom to sell. His marketplace is the television screen, modern music, popular magazines and newspapers, and current books. He even sets up shop in the home and in the church. When we buy into that unspiritual wisdom, we open ourselves to envy, selfish ambition, disorder, and countless evil practices. And those, in turn, feed the turmoil in which the human race is caught. Let us thank God for "the wisdom that comes from heaven"—what a lovely

description! Let us pray that we may diligently cultivate divine wisdom and regularly root out the weeds and thorns of devilish wisdom.

Watering

Read James 1:5.

After promising us wisdom, James reminds us that we must ask for that wisdom in faith. But let us concentrate, for the time being, on verse 5. It is an echo of Jesus' more general promise, "Ask and it will be given to you" (Matthew 7:7). With Jesus' promise, we know that there are some requests that are unlikely to be granted. If we ask for a million dollars, for total avoidance of sickness or sorrow, or for a reversal of the aging process, we are not likely to get what we asked for. But God wants us all to have the spiritual wisdom James describes, so we can pray for it with confidence. Let us thank God for this simple promise regarding prayer for wisdom. Let us pray for a clearer realization of God's generosity toward us.

NOTES

Week 46

Growing the crop of

STRONGER FAITH IN GOD

The *Amplified Bible* is sometimes helpful in comprehending the various shades of meaning in the Hebrew and Greek words chosen by the original writers of Scripture. For example, consider what Paul and Silas said to the Philippian jailer in Acts 16:31: "Believe in the Lord Jesus Christ—that is, give yourself up to him, take yourself out of your own keeping and entrust yourself into his keeping, and you will be saved."

When we seek faith, we must seek it in all its biblical richness. We must surrender. We must put aside any pretense of our own sufficiency. We must wholly lean upon the saving and sustaining power of God. The Scriptures we will sow this week will aid us in doing that.

Plowing
Read Ezekiel 33:10, 11.

The people of Israel seemed to be saying, "We are sinning, and it is ruining us, but we cannot do anything about it." But God through Ezekiel answered, "Yes, you can do something about it. Turn away from your sins!" Today we also may protest, "I cannot help myself. Temptation is too strong, and I am too weak." Yet God is still telling us we can change, and he will provide the power to do it. Let us thank God for showing us that his power is stronger than self, sin, and Satan. Let us pray that we may open up our minds and hearts to that overcoming power.

Sowing
Read Hebrews 11:1-6.

Hebrews 11 is appropriately called "the faith chapter of the Bible." It offers various examples of people who pleased God because they came to him believing "that he exists and that he rewards those who earnestly seek him." Faith does not come to those who merely pray for it. But meditating on these examples of faith and praying that they will inspire us to a like faith will certainly help. Let us thank God for people like Enoch, Noah, Abraham, and Moses and for their active, victorious faith. Let us pray that we will learn to use the Word of God effectively as a tool to strengthen our faith.

Cultivating
Read 1 John 5:1-5.

We sing "Faith Is the Victory," but is our faith truly the overcoming, victorious kind of faith? Or would we have to admit that it is flabby, feeble, and faltering? There is nothing complicated about faith. It is a matter of believing "that Jesus is the Son of God." We may say we believe that, but is our belief a dynamic, vibrant, compelling force within us? That is the faith for which we must aim; that is the faith that overcomes. Let us thank God for the abundant evidence in Scripture that Jesus is indeed the Son of God. Let us pray for guidance in sowing and cultivating that truth in our hearts so that it will produce the harvest of a victorious faith.

Cultivating
Read Romans 10:9-17.

The *King James Version* renders verse 17 as follows: "So then, faith cometh by hearing, and hearing by the word of God." By using this book to study some significant passages in the Word of God, we are building faith; reaping faith; strengthening faith. And it is important to emphasize that the more we sow and cultivate Scripture, the greater will be our harvest of faith. Let us thank God for his faith-building Word. Let us pray for the wisdom to give God's Word a high priority in our schedules.

Watering
Read Proverbs 3:5, 6.

The Bible frequently emphasizes that a right relationship with God is an "all your heart" kind of situation. This is where the Bible and prayer are so valuable. We do not worship a god made of wood, stone, or precious metal. We must not lavish our wholehearted attention and devotion on any material objects. But we can give wholehearted attention to Bible study and prayer. By so doing, we are able to seek God, trust God, and love God with all our hearts. Let us thank God that we can trust him with all our hearts and acknowledge him in all our ways. Let us pray that we will learn to use the Bible and prayer effectively in accomplishing these goals.

NOTES

Week 47

Growing the crop of

SUBMISSION TO GOD'S WILL

Perhaps this simple prayer that I have used at the beginning of many days will help others:

Lord, give me strength today,
And guide my steps, I pray,
To walk your chosen way
In all I do and say.

I yield my life to you,
My time and talents, too.
And when this day is through,
Give rest; my soul renew.

Work it in with prayers related to the Scriptures for this week, and let God work his perfect will in you.

Plowing
Read Ezekiel 14:6-8.

What an appropriate description: a man who "sets up idols in his heart." This fits the Old Testament practice of making idols of wood, stone, or metal. It also is applicable to our time, when idols take the form of homes, automobiles, recreational vehicles, and other possessions. How we need to echo William Cowper's prayer: "The dearest idol I have known,/ Whate'er that idol be,/ Help me to tear it from Thy throne/ And worship only Thee." Let us thank God for the material possessions he has enabled us to obtain. But let us also pray that we may avoid the worship of possessions or the temptation to put our trust in them.

Sowing
Read Matthew 6:9-13.

We have probably uttered the words of the Lord's Prayer dozens, perhaps hundreds, of times. Have we merely recited it, or have we made it a personal prayer? When we say, "Your will be done on earth as it is in heaven," we should, in effect, be praying, "O God, work your will on earth, beginning in me. Help me first of all to do your will with the same promptness and joy as the angels. Then help me to influence others to perform your will in the same way." Let us thank God for the Lord's Prayer, so magnificent in its brevity and comprehensiveness. Let us pray that we may better appreciate how God's will is done in Heaven and that we may learn to do it similarly on earth.

Cultivating
Read Ephesians 6:5-8.

It is not very appealing to picture ourselves as slaves to another human being. But to be a slave of Jesus Christ—that is another matter.

To see Jesus Christ alone as our master, to dedicate every word and every action to the accomplishment of his service how much easier then could we be "doing the will of God from [our] heart." Let us thank God for this glorious privilege of being a slave of his Son. Let us pray for a clearer vision of what this blessed slavery involves.

Cultivating
Read Matthew 12:46-50.

It is tempting to envy Mary for all those years of closeness to Jesus. It is easy to feel exasperation toward Jesus' brothers for their obstinate refusal to recognize that they were living in the same family as the Son of God. But we can experience a closeness to Jesus no less intimate than his earthly family did. We need only to open our eyes to that fellowship and friendship with him that lies within reach of all who will embrace the Father's will. Let us thank God for making his will for us clear, and thus extending to us a means of closeness to his Son. Let us pray that we may move more into the center of the divine will and thereby know Jesus Christ more intimately.

Watering
Read Psalm 143:10.

Teach me to do your will." It is surely a prayer that God delights to hear, a prayer that he is pleased to answer. Of course, it must be offered in sincerity, and it can be, if we will simply get it into our heads that God's will is at all times what is best for us. God desires to lead us "on level ground," to guide us in the way of godly success. Let us thank God for his perfect will for us and for his readiness to teach us that will. Let us pray that we may indeed understand that what God wants for us is what will benefit us most.

NOTES

Week 48

Growing the crop of

THANKSGIVING TO GOD

T hanksgiving is not merely a holiday. It is an attitude and a practice that we should observe year-round, day by day. It is a lifestyle that recognizes the smallest of blessings and is equally content in abundance or need.

It is easy to be thankful on Thanksgiving Day. It is a day away from work. Family is near. There is food in abundance.

But God continually supplies us with blessings. Do we thank him daily for our jobs, our homes, our health, freedom in the nation in which we live, and the beauty of nature? When we ponder this, we must conclude that every day is Thanksgiving Day. The Bible passages for this week will help us remember God's benefits and our reasons for continual thanksgiving.

Plowing
Read Proverbs 1:22-27.

The *New International Version* adds a footnote pointing out how the word "simple" in this passage implies an inclination to immorality and evil. To some extent, we are all simple in this way. If we are to benefit from the Word of God, we must consciously turn away from every inclination toward evil and respond to God's call to righteousness. Let us thank God that we have the power to choose his ways rather than evil. Let us pray that God will "plow up" these inclinations to think and to do what is immoral and ungodly.

Sowing
Read Psalm 100:1-5.

In this psalm, the psalmist enumerates several reasons why we should be thankful to God. God has made us; God is good to us; God loves us; God is faithful to us. We can profitably echo the praises expressed in this psalm. Let us indeed thank God not only for making us but also for making us his people. Let us pray that we may perceive more clearly his goodness, love, and faithfulness and that we may make these a constant theme in our thanksgiving.

Cultivating
Read Romans 1:18-23.

The evidence of God's existence and power is all around us, and the good things for which we should be thanking God are clearly seen. These include sunshine and rain, the air we breathe, our food and water, and much more. Yet, like the people of whom Paul writes, many today fail to glorify God or give thanks to him. How desperately do people need to have their eyes opened! Let us thank God for those basic gifts we have mentioned, gifts that all human beings enjoy. Let us pray for the opening of human eyes everywhere to the magnificence of God's provision.

Cultivating
Read Luke 17:11-19.

It may seem negative to focus on the nine ungrateful lepers rather than the one who thanked Jesus. However, the reaction of the nine to their healing is very much typical of human beings today. We whine over bad times, and we quickly forget the Source of our blessings when they come. Thanksgiving must be a more consistent practice. Let us thank God right now for what we have been taking for granted: our families, our health, our jobs, and all the good things we enjoy. Let us prayerfully acknowledge that even in tough times we have much for which to be thankful.

Watering
Read 1 Thessalonians 5:18.

Consider some alternatives to this verse: "Become angry in all circumstances." "Protect your pride in all circumstances." "Complain in all circumstances." We may feel that we could more easily obey one or more of these than "Give thanks in all circumstances." How can we give thanks when our car will not start, when our furnace breaks down, or when our body temperature soars over the one-hundred degree mark? It is a matter of developing a habit, a very worthwhile habit. Let us thank God for the lofty challenge to which this verse calls us. Let us pray for God's guidance in developing this habitual thanksgiving.

NOTES

Week 49

Growing the crop of

TRUTHFULNESS

The story of George Washington's cutting down the cherry tree and honestly admitting to his father that he did it once inspired the nation's children to truthfulness. Today many children and adults would laugh at such a story. The very existence of truth is questioned in our society. Advertisers choose words carefully to highlight benefits of their products while obscuring their deficiencies. Truth seems to be defined today as telling only what will work to your advantage.

But there is still such a thing as objective truth. We are still obligated to give an accurate, factual account of what has happened. That is what God wants, and that is what we need to reproduce in human affairs.

Plowing
Read 1 Kings 8:46-51.

This is part of the tremendous prayer Solomon offered at the dedication of the temple. He asked simply that God would hear the prayers of penitent sinners, taken from Israel into a land of captivity. He prayed that the Lord would forgive them and cause their captors to treat them kindly. We will, I hope, never experience the destruction of our homeland and exile into another country. But we may, on account of sin, become separated from our families, our friends, our churches and our God. May God also hear our prayers of repentance! Let us thank God that he is never so far away that he cannot hear our penitent pleas. Let us pray that we will not carelessly separate ourselves from him.

Sowing
Read Proverbs 12:17-22.

How many different ways can it be said that God treasures truthfulness and loathes lying? These days we have some clever ways of excusing lying. The government speaks of "disinformation," while we talk about "little white lies" or "stretching the truth." God takes this matter of truthfulness much more seriously than we do. Let us thank God for his delight in truthfulness. Let us pray that we may see the practice of lying from God's vantage point and that we may come to hate it as much as he does.

Cultivating
Read Zephaniah 3:9-13.

No lies, no deceit—this was part of Zephaniah's vision of a purified people. And it is an aspect of his vision that we may find especially appealing. How much confusion and conflict have we experienced because of lies and deceit? Perhaps we ourselves have woven "the tangled web" of deceit or have become enmeshed in the problems caused by the lies of others. It is pleasant to envision a time when perfect truthfulness will banish all lies and deceit. Let us thank God for the challenge of practicing complete truthfulness. Let us pray for divine discomfort any time we are tempted to digress from the truth.

Cultivating
Read Ephesians 4:25-32.

It is surely true that the human tongue is one of the greatest barriers to harmony and growth in the church. Whether we call it lying or "telling our side of the story," we sometimes distort what some brother or sister has said or done. We speak out in anger or whisper our slanders and in such ways try to salve our wounded ego by inflicting hurt on the one whom we feel has hurt us. Let us thank God for forgiving us all our sins, including those we have committed with our tongue. Let

us pray that he will help us transform our tongues into instruments of blessing rather than weapons of destruction.

Watering
Read Exodus 20:16.

This command is not limited to a court of law. No doubt God is displeased any time we do damage to another person through lies, slander, or misrepresentation. In fact, God is displeased enough that he made the prohibition of false testimony one of the Ten Commandments. Even though the command we are dealing with here is in the Old Testament, the New Testament makes it clear that God's attitude toward this sin has not changed. (See Colossians 3:8, 9; Revelation 21:8; 22:15.) Let us thank God for his many reminders of our obligation to our neighbors and to the truth. Let us pray that we may better understand the damage false testimony can do to human beings and that we may thereby be determined to avoid it.

NOTES

Week 50

Growing the crop of

VICTORY OVER FEAR

Consider some of the ways fear hurts us: it produces mental turmoil and physical tension; it robs us of joy and chills our enthusiasm; it hinders us from performing our duty and pressures us into running from responsibility; it erodes our trust in God and our love for him.

But how can we rid ourselves of fear's tenacious grip? Must we resort to the psychiatrist's couch, to mind-altering drugs, or to humanistic self-help formulas?

Surely God's Word offers us the most powerful antidote to fear. Let us utilize the Scriptures for this week to weed out poisonous fear and to grow a healthy sense of confidence in God, his love, and his power.

Plowing
Read 2 Chronicles 15:1-4.

Here is the benefit of distress: it led Israel to seek the Lord and to find him. Throughout the centuries, that has been an often-repeated pattern. When proud, self-sufficient human beings encounter pain, grief, fear, frustration, defeat, and distress, they often begin to seek the Lord. Has that happened to us? Let us thank God for those trials that lead us to look away from ourselves and toward him. Let us pray for the ability to discern his gracious hand in our trials and for the wisdom to respond with faith and obedience.

Sowing
Read Psalm 91:1-8.

Is the psalmist promising an absolute escape from all harm for the believer? That cannot be the case. It would be out of harmony with the experiences of believers in both the Old and New Testament eras. The psalmist's words are surely intended, rather, to give us confidence that God will sustain and support us in any trial. If God is with us, as he has promised to be, then we need not fear any possible crisis. Let us thank God that the Bible is filled with such promises. Let us pray that our faith will increasingly prevail over our fears.

Cultivating
Read Hebrews 2:14-18.

How much human fear is rooted in the fear of death? Could we say, "If I were absolutely convinced that there is abundant life after death, nothing would make me afraid"? Jesus came to free us from enslavement to the fear of death, so we must be capable of developing an unshakable confidence in our personal resurrection and victory over death. Let us thank God that he has provided such a freedom from the fear of death. Let us pray that the devil's influence over us in connection with this fear will be broken.

Watering
Read Romans 8:15.

Cultivating
Read 1 John 4:17-21.

How do we react to fear? We try to avoid it; we psychoanalyze it; we dull its insistent voice with drugs or alcohol; we grit our teeth and try to face it. Here the Bible tells us the only effective way to drive out fear. Perfect love is the answer. How do we acquire this perfect love? We meditate on the truth that "God is love," as this chapter earlier declares. Then we pray for God's perfect love and trust him to send his love to drive out our fear. Let us thank God for placing perfect love within our reach. Let us also pray that we may better understand how "God is love" and then let his fear-banishing love dwell within us.

Many preachers, teachers, and writers have called attention to the fact that the Aramaic word "Abba" was an intimate and tender way of addressing a father. So we see that, through the Holy Spirit, we enjoy an intimate relationship with our heavenly Father. Like the frightened child who climbs up onto his father's lap, we can go to our Father and have our fearfulness calmed. Let us thank God for this intimate relationship with our Father in Heaven. Let us pray that we may learn to take our fears promptly to him.

NOTES

Week 51

Growing the crop of

WAITING ON AND HOPING IN GOD

Hope springs eternal in the human breast." So goes the familiar observation. But hope seems to be running dry in many human breasts today.

Perhaps that is because hope has been based on crumbling and inadequate foundations. Hope that rests only on human strength and ingenuity, on money and possessions, on charismatic human leadership, and on science and technology is doomed to failure.

But we may hope in God and wait upon him, and that is a hope founded in eternal truth and power. The following passages can aid us in sowing patience, faith, and hope in our hearts.

Plowing
Read Hosea 10:12.

Unplowed ground—packed down hard by many seasons of beating rains and baking sunshine. Unplowed ground—where only the hardiest weeds can force their roots down into the soil. Have your heart and mind been like this—hard and resistant to God's grace? "Break up your unplowed ground!" Soften your heart to receive his word; yield your will so that he can make you like a fruitful field. Let us thank God for his goodness and patience toward us in spite of our inclination to hardness. Let us pray that we may be aware of any remaining "unplowed ground" in our hearts and yield it up to him.

Sowing
Read Psalm 130:1-8.

The psalmist was committed to waiting: "I wait for the LORD, my soul waits, and in his word I put my hope." In spite of his obvious depression, crying out of the depths, the psalmist was prepared to wait on God to deliver in his own way and in his own time. Let us thank God for his wisdom in controlling the timing of our blessings and our victories over certain problems. Let us pray that we shall learn to appreciate the wisdom of his timing and then accept it.

Cultivating
Read Isaiah 40:27-31.

We marvel sometimes at the basketball player who runs tirelessly from one end of the court to the other. We are equally amazed at the long-distance runner who keeps up a measured pace through most of five thousand meters but is still able to summon extra energy for a closing kick. This passage in Isaiah seems to promise such physical stamina. But perhaps we should interpret it as referring to spiritual vibrancy. However, it is true that what we do with our hearts and minds affects the energy level of our bodies. Let us thank God that he does not grow weary of hearing our prayers and mightily ministering to our needs. Let us pray that we will so hope in the Lord as to renew our spiritual and physical strength and to soar above the tendency to weariness of soul and body.

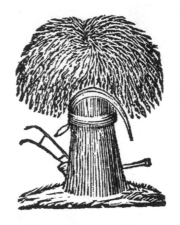

Cultivating
Read Isaiah 26:7-11.

Yes, LORD, walking in the way of your laws, we wait for you." This prayer shows us clearly that waiting on God does not imply idleness. Instead, we wait on God by actively pursuing obedience, holiness, and service according to his word. As we so walk, we wait for God to supply the strength and direction we need. Let us thank God that he has shown us positive things to do while we wait for him. Let us pray that we shall develop the determination to shun idleness, undue hesitancy, and ingenious excuses and get to work.

Watering
Read Psalm 27:13, 14.

What a statement of faith David made! In spite of the dangers his enemies posed, he could declare, "I am still confident of this: I will see the goodness of the LORD in the land of the living." That stands in stark contrast to the "Oh, woe is me!" kind of attitude we are tempted to take. Let us thank God that he has given us cause to believe that we shall at last prevail over troubling circumstances. Let us pray that we shall "be strong and take heart," so that we can avoid a spirit of whining and complaining as we wait on God.

NOTES

Week 52

Growing the crop of

ZEAL

Whatever one may think of the writings of the late Norman Vincent Peale, the title of one of his books is surely accurate: *Enthusiasm Makes the Difference*. Difficult work becomes easier when it is done with enthusiasm. Repetitious tasks tend to go faster when we put some zeal into them. Any kind of labor performed not grudgingly, but zestfully, is likely to be more productive.

This is as true of our spiritual duties as it is of our toil in the workplace and in the home. Zeal and enthusiasm seem to come naturally to some people, but most of us will need to grow it with the help of God's Word. That is the goal of our study this week.

Plowing
Read Hosea 14:1, 2.

Downfall"—what a frightening word! Have we already suffered a downfall because of sin, or are we on the brink of such a downfall? It is time to humble ourselves before the Lord and ask for forgiveness, healing, and restoration. Let us take words of penitence, words of confession, words of submission to God and return to the One who wants to forgive. Let us thank God for his wonderful willingness to forgive. Let us pray that our downfall or near-downfall will become God's instrument in restoring us to fellowship with him.

Sowing
Read Mark 5:1-20.

The man who had been demon-possessed must have become a zealous spokesman for Jesus. He amazed the citizens of the Decapolis (ten Greek cities) by his report of what had happened to him. We can imagine his exclamations: "Jesus healed me! He is more powerful than the devil! He is surely the Son of God! Everyone should follow him!" Let us thank God for our reason to be zealous: how much the Lord has done for us and how he has had mercy on us. Let us pray that we may channel our zeal into effective witness and service for our Lord.

Cultivating
Read Acts 18:24-28.

For the moment, let us overlook the fact that Apollos possessed a deficient knowledge of spiritual truth when he first appears in Acts. Let us instead focus on the evidences of his zeal— "he spoke with great fervor"; "he began to speak boldly"; "he vigorously refuted the Jews." Oh, to possess such a burning zeal! Most of us have an abundance of biblical knowledge, and if we could combine it with an Apollos-like zeal, we could be power-houses for the gospel. Let us thank God for the zeal of Apollos and for his readiness to have that zeal properly focused. Let us pray that, as we grow in knowledge, we may experience an equal growth in the intensity of our spiritual fervor.

Cultivating
Read Revelation 3:14-22.

Here is a sermon in a cup of water. If it is hot, put a teabag or a spoonful of instant coffee or cocoa in it and enjoy a body-warming beverage. If it is cold, drink it as is or with lemon, grape, or some other flavoring in it and be refreshed. But if it is luke-warm, throw it out! We can

imagine how disgusting luke-warm disciples must be to the Lord. Let us be hot, boiling, steaming in our zeal for his cause. Let us thank God for Jesus' gentle invitation to fel-lowship with him—how can we be lukewarm about that? Let us pray that we will share our Lord's disgust over any lukewarmness in his church and that we will be willing to "heat up" our zeal.

Watering
Read Romans 12:11.

Here is a situation in which a high tempera-ture is desirable. A body temperature of over one hundred can signal a prob-lem, and we should take action to lower it. But our "zeal temperature" must always remain high. The word "fervor" resembles "fever," which can remind us to be in a state of constant fever as we serve the Lord. Let us thank God for the means of keeping our zeal for the gospel stirred to a fever pitch. Let us pray that we will never allow affliction or indif-ference to cool our zeal.

NOTES

INDEX